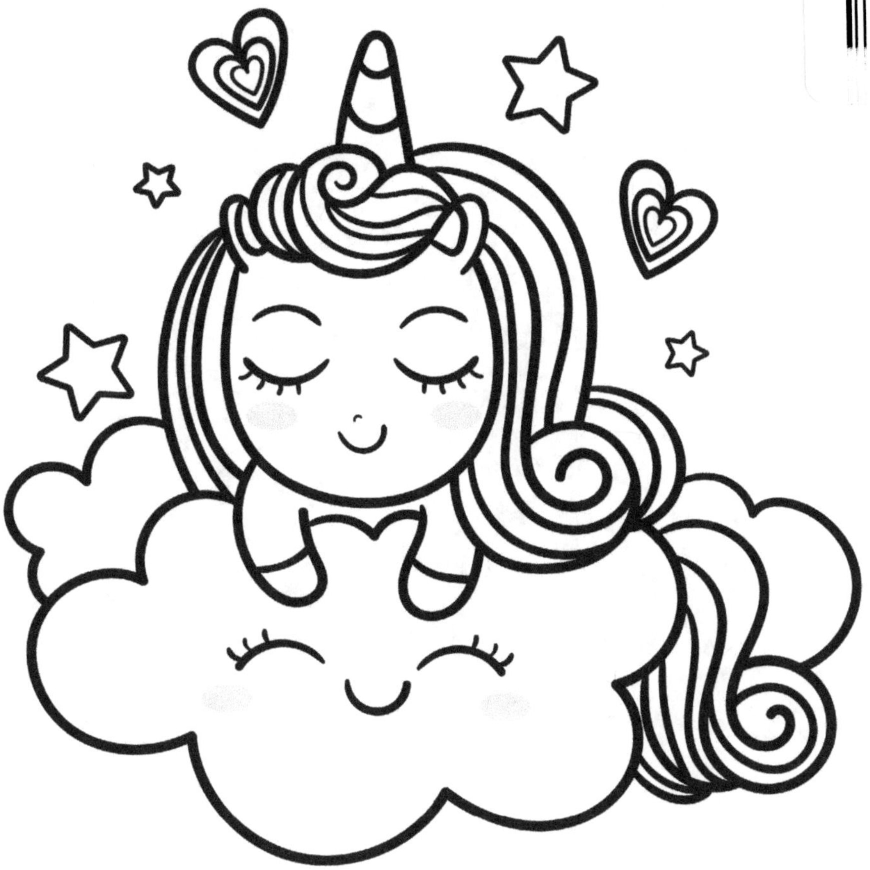

UNICORN

COLORING BOOK FOR KIDS AGES 2-8

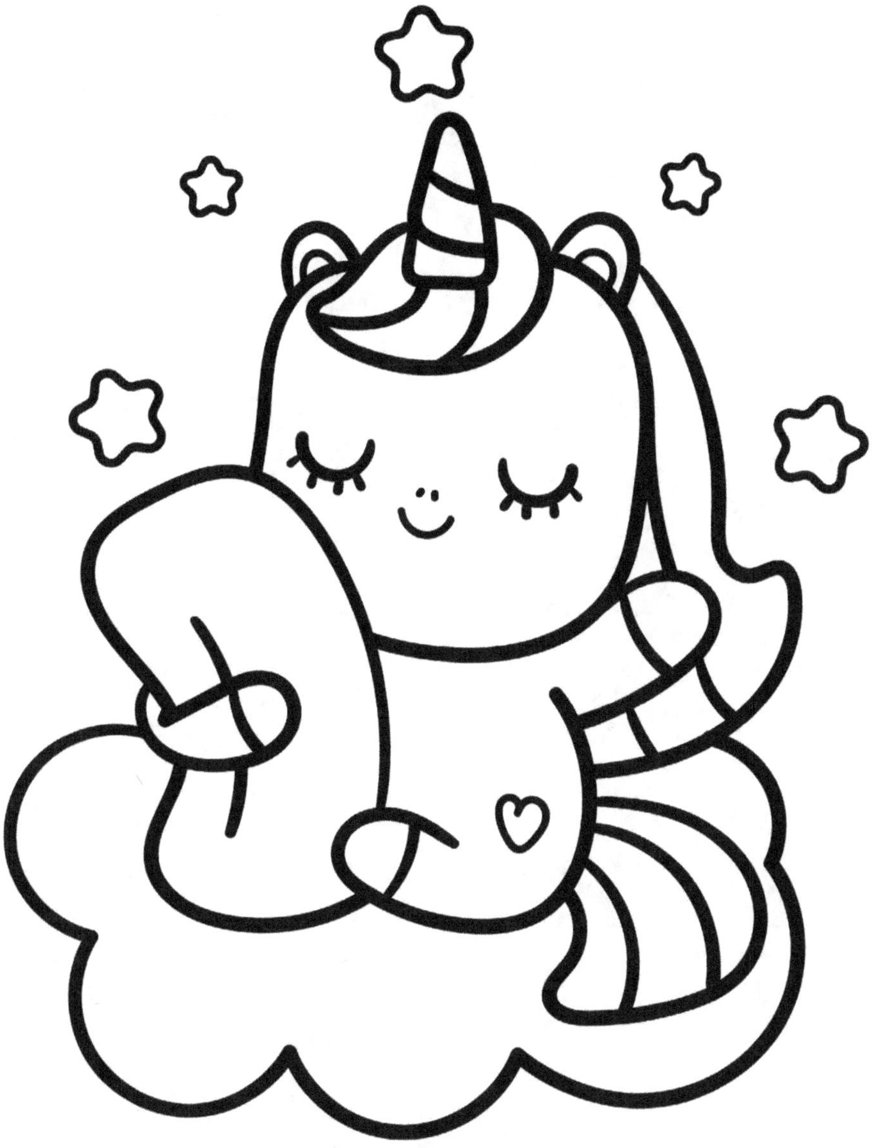

THIS BOOK
BELONGS TO

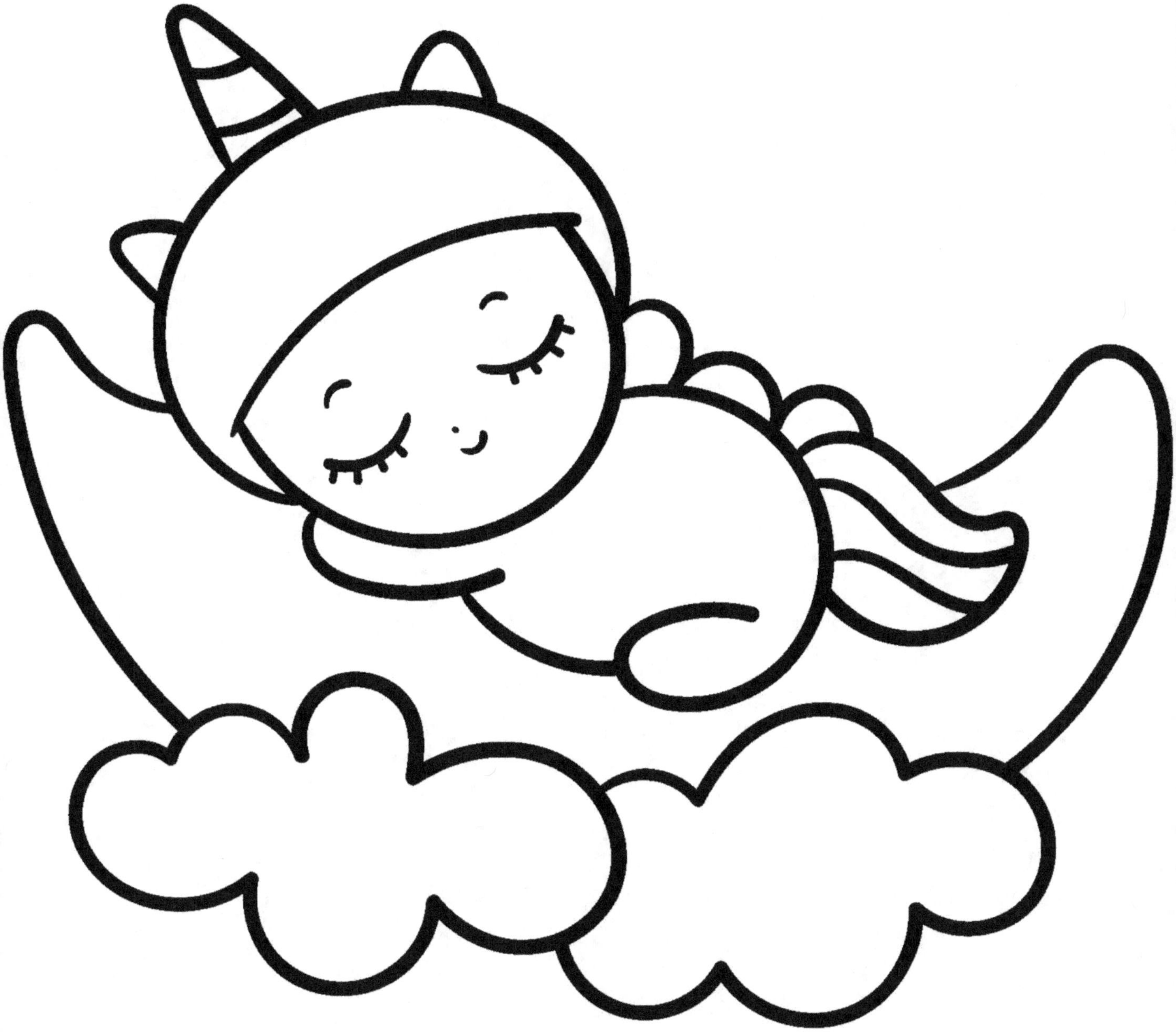

Sweet Dream

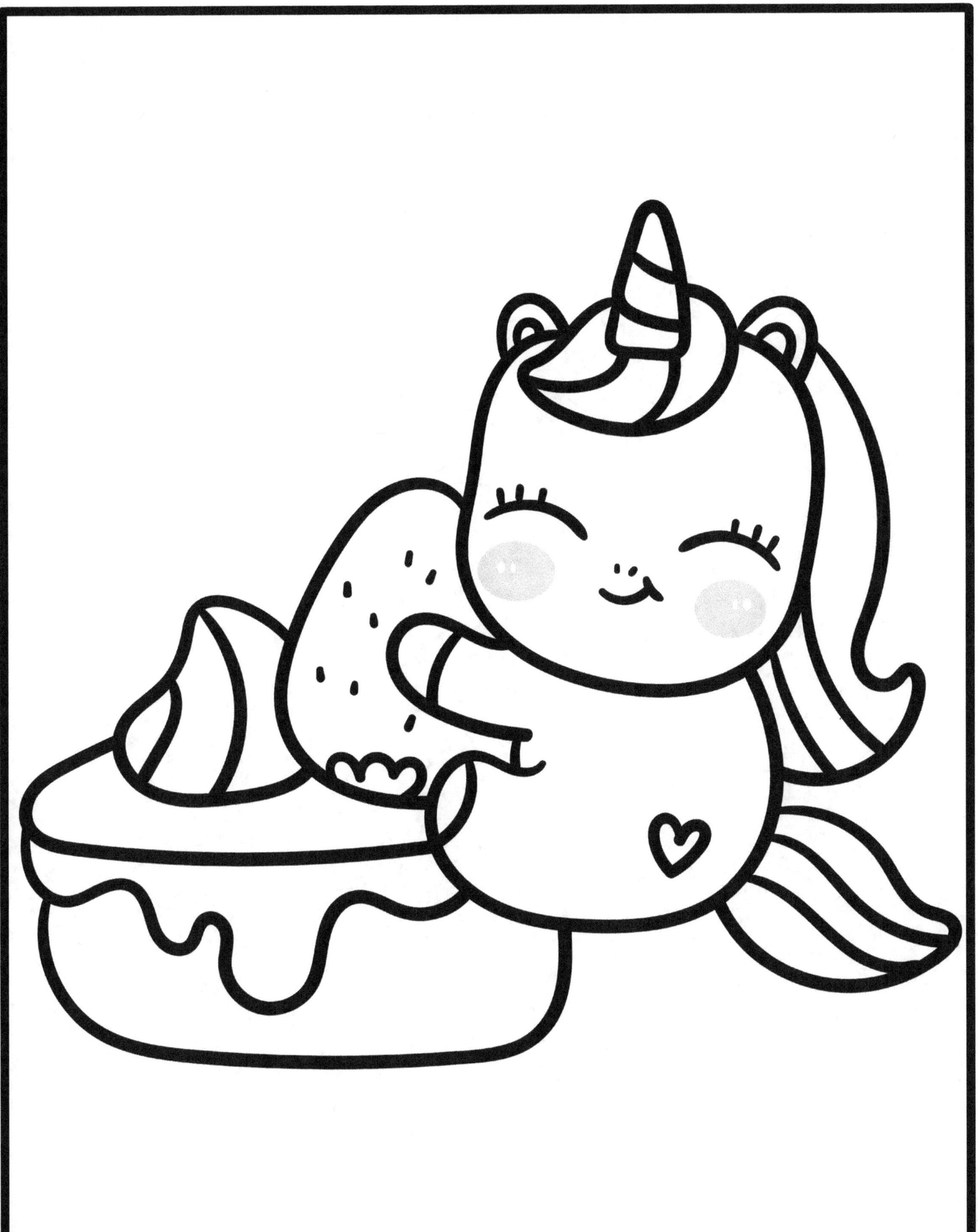

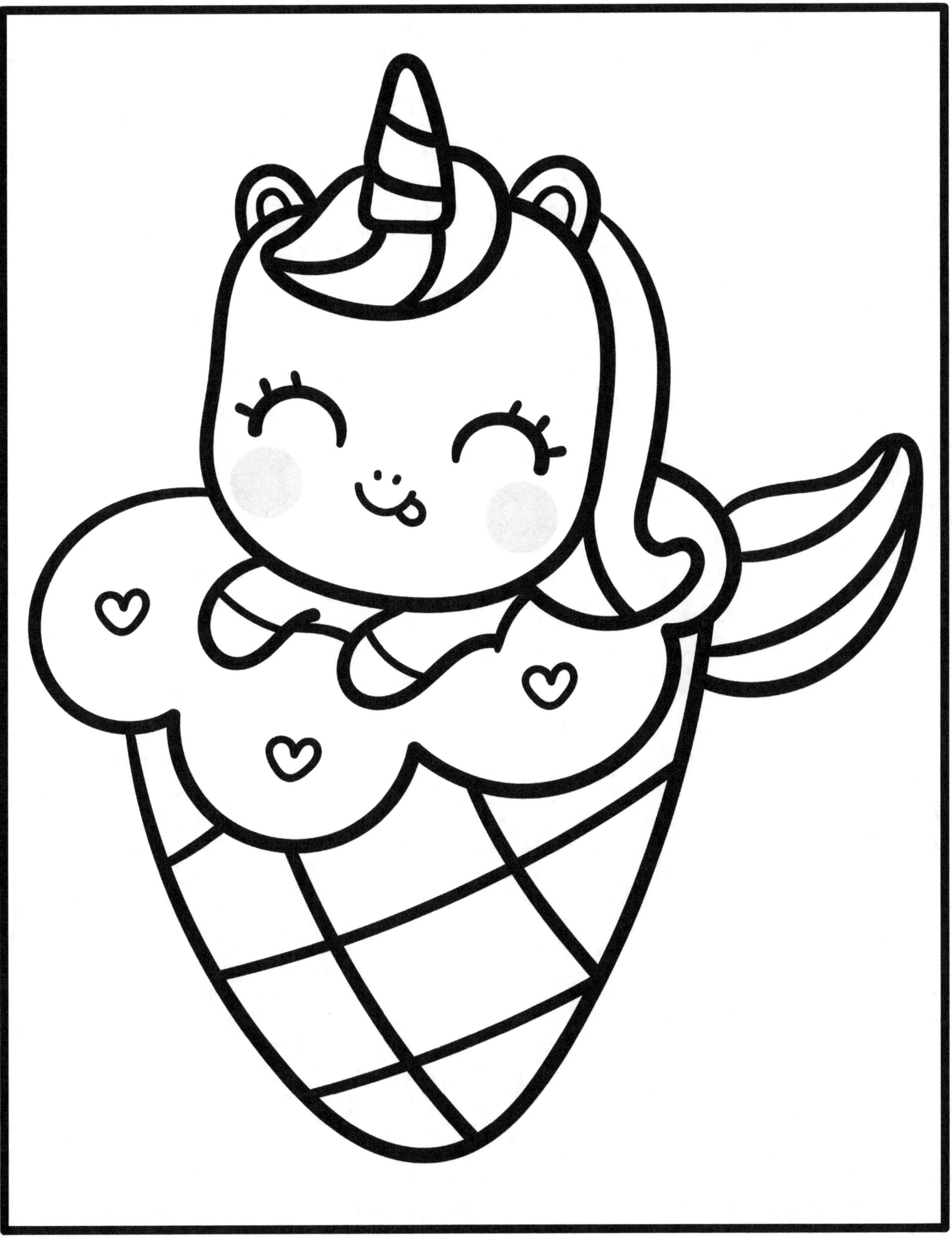

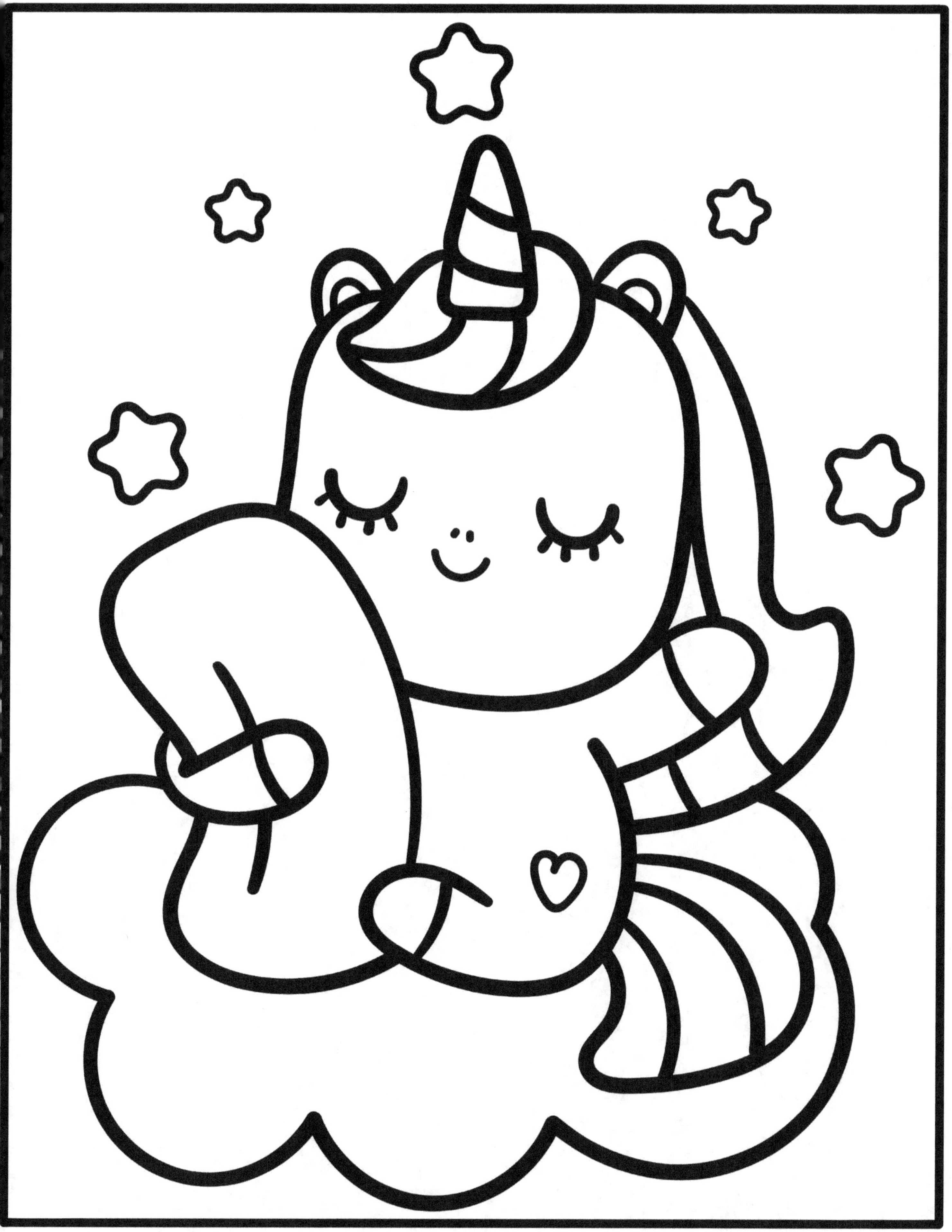

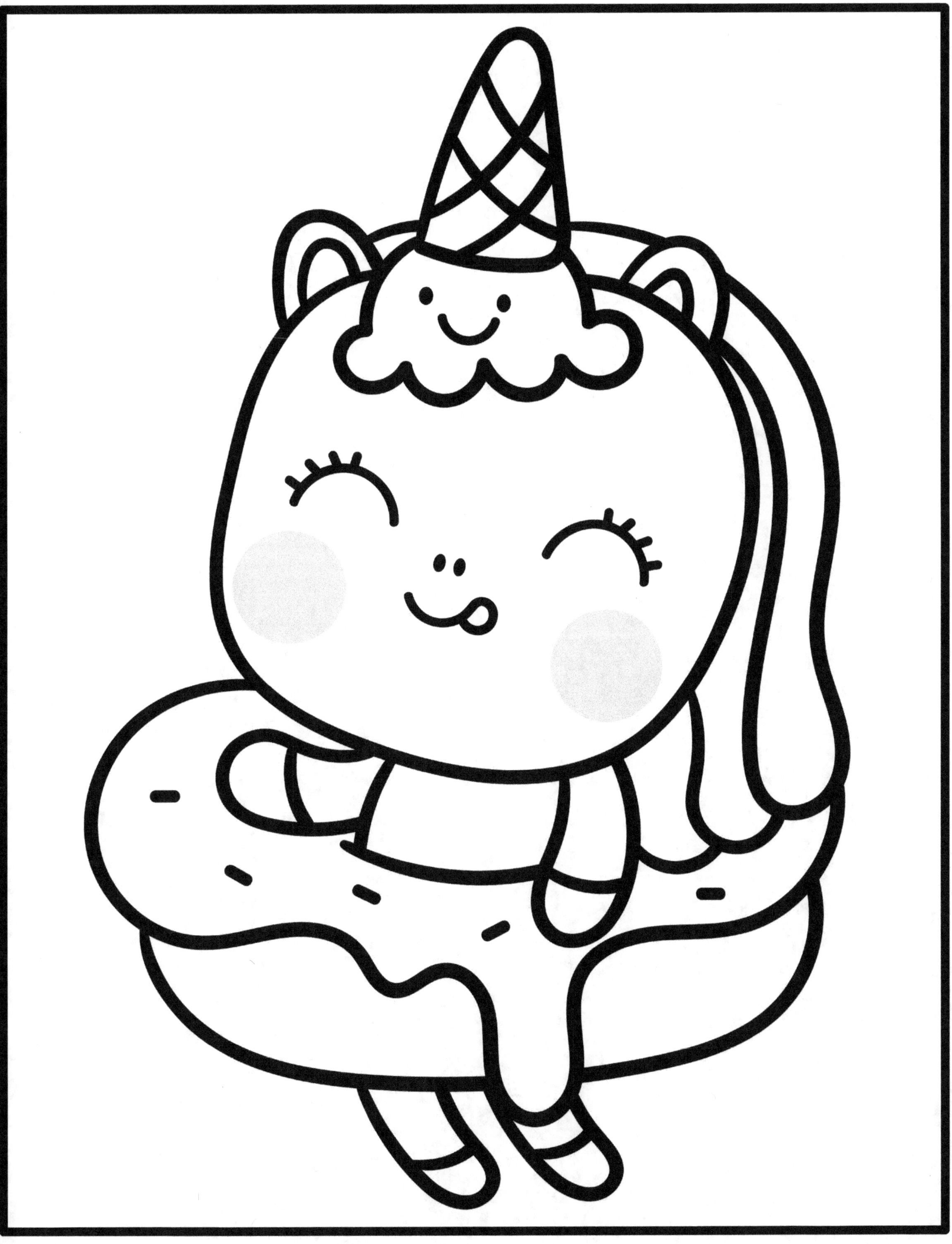

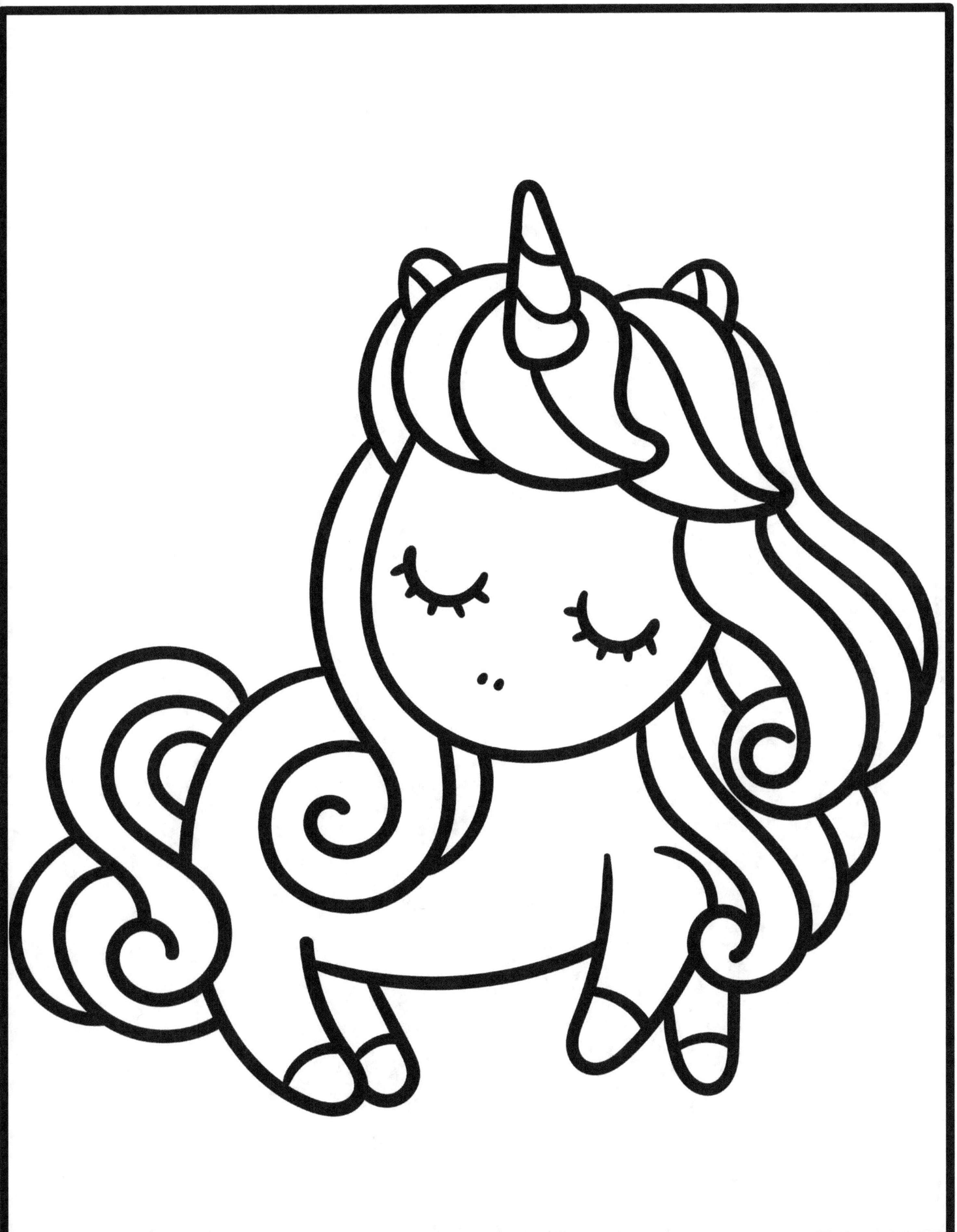

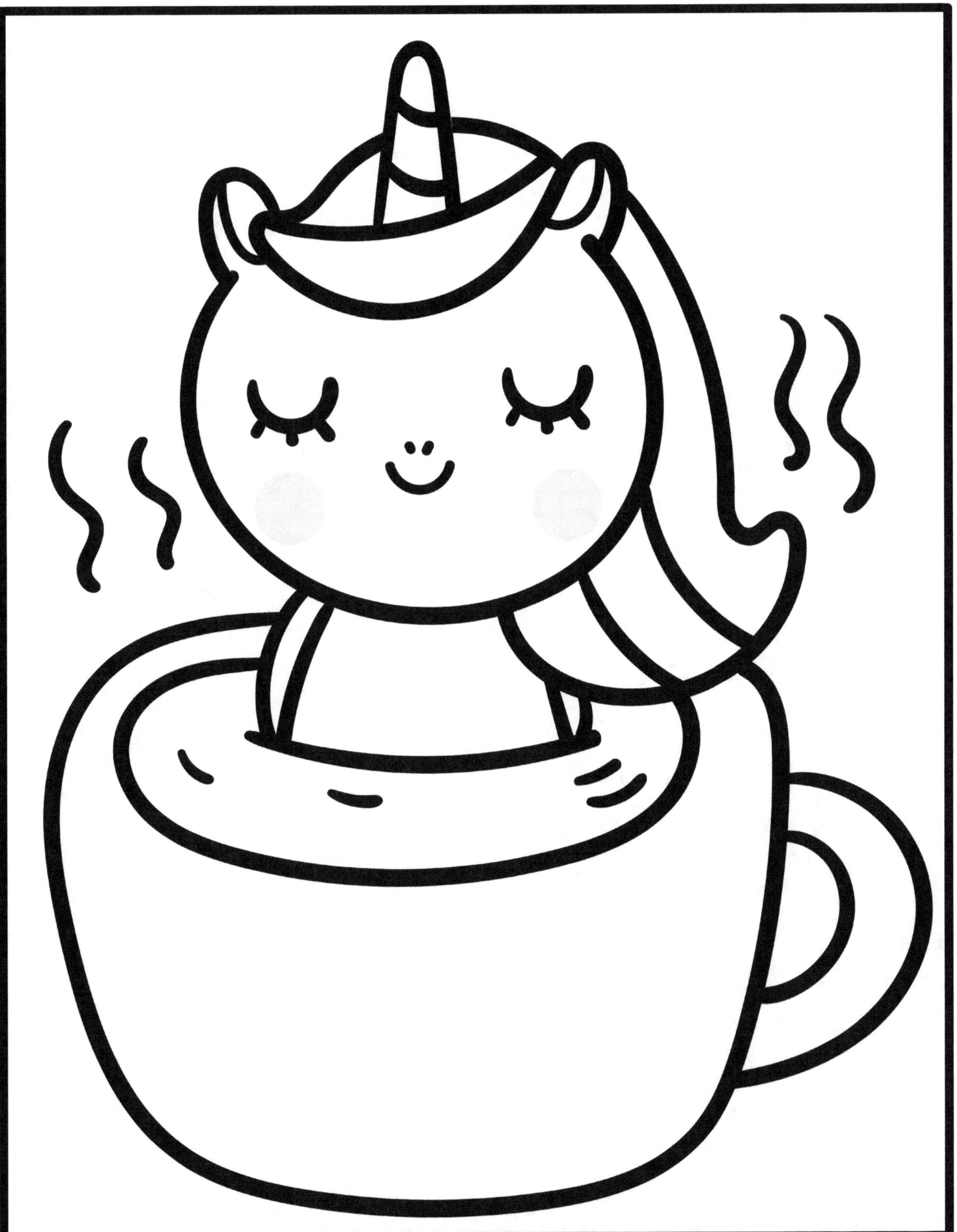

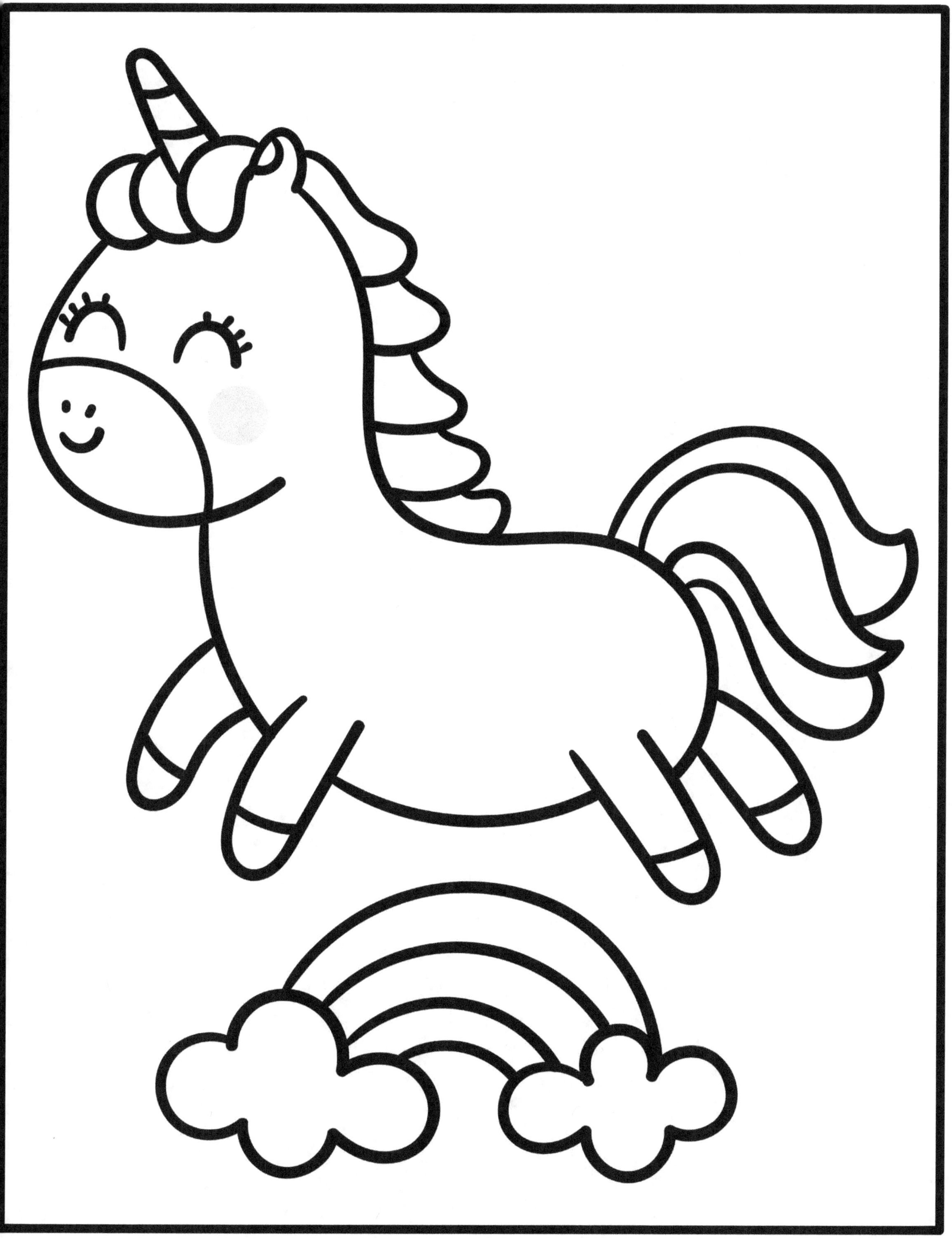

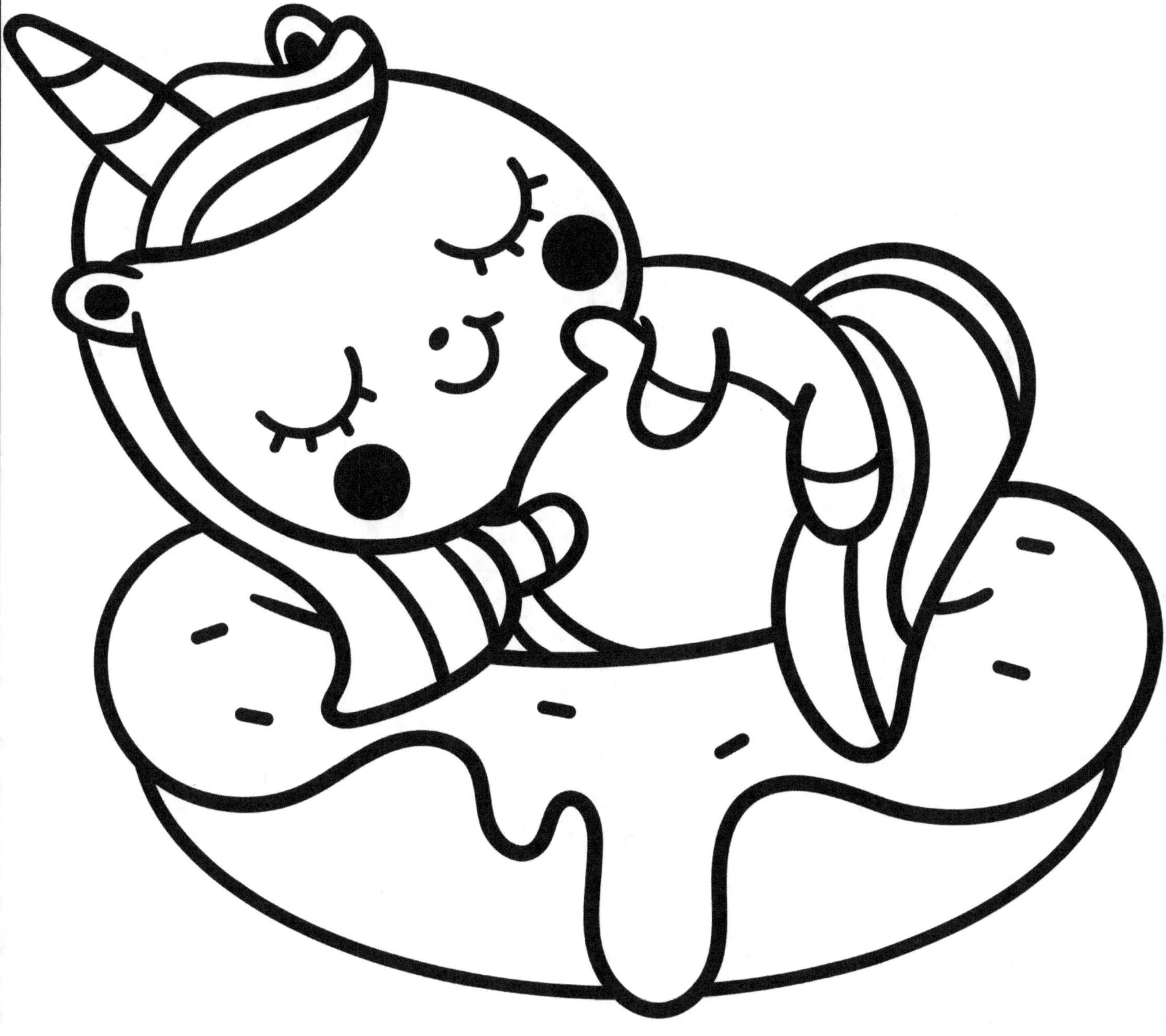

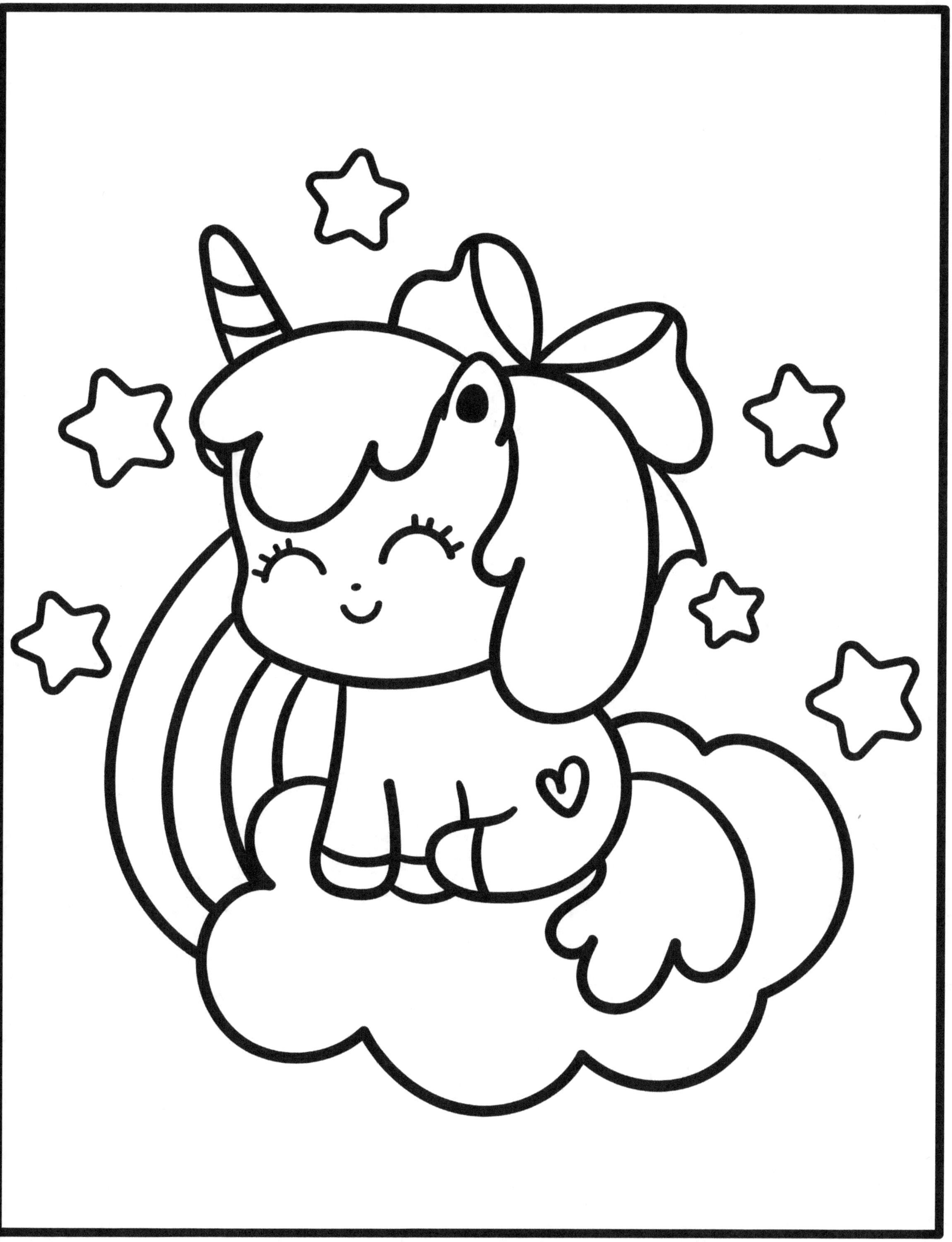

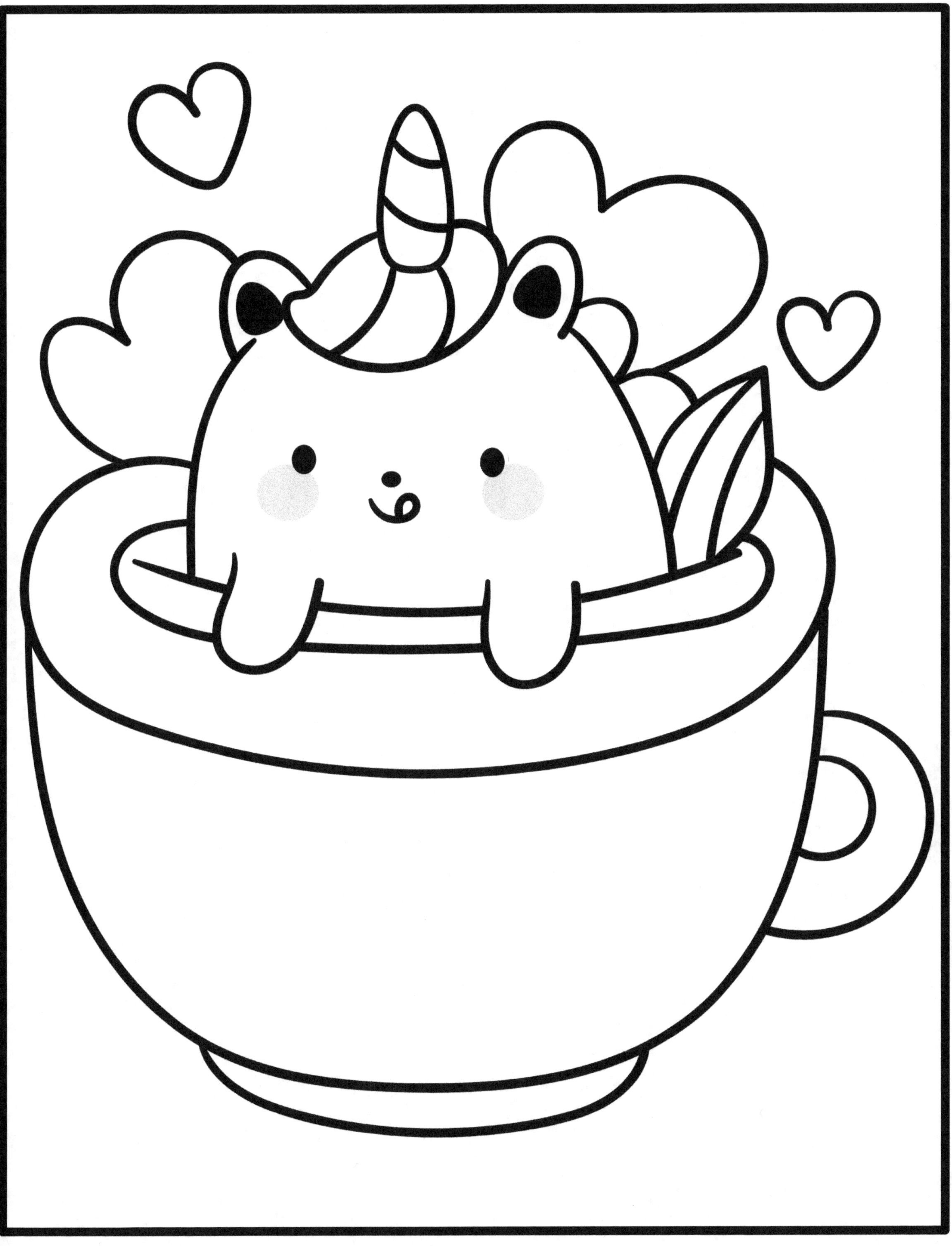

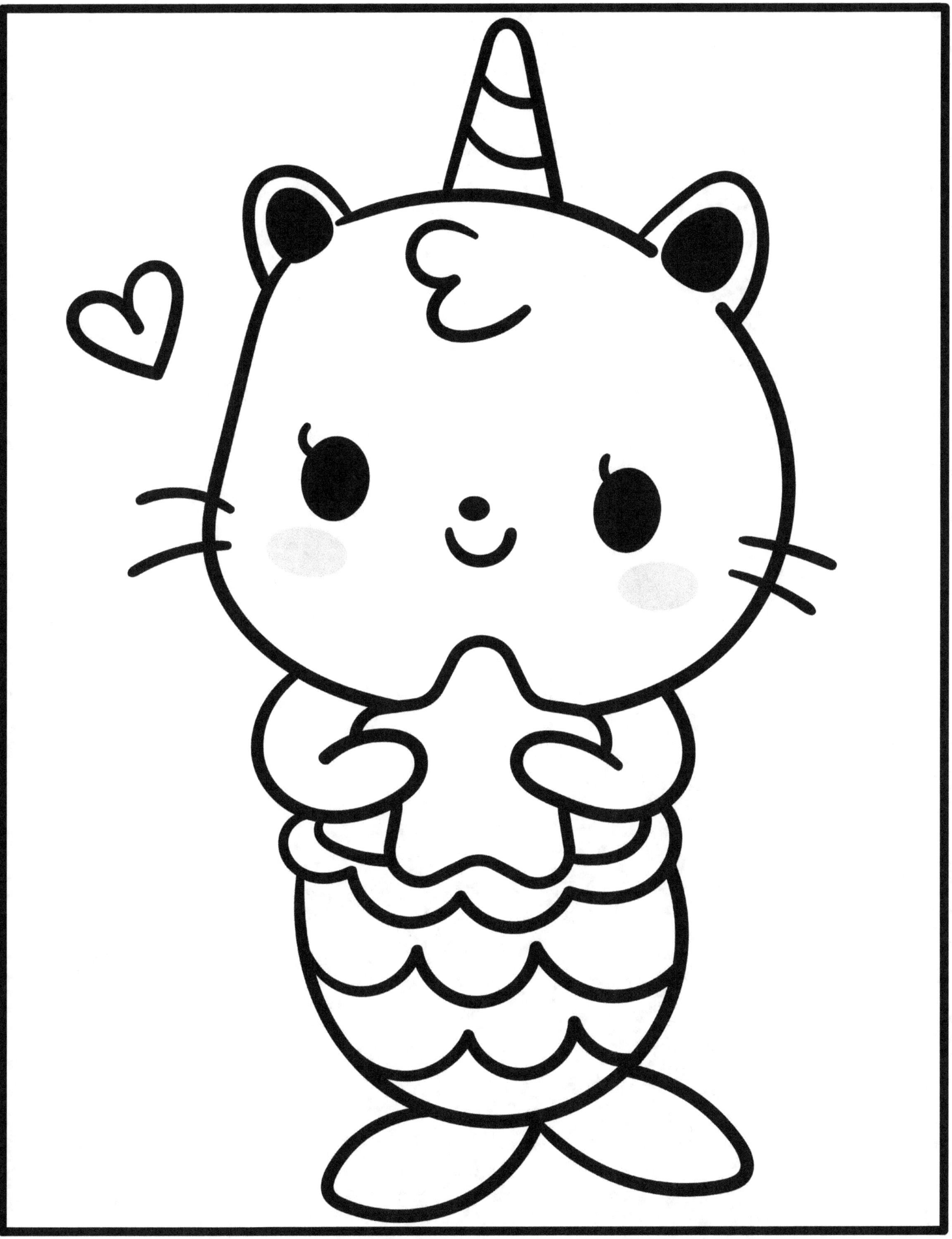

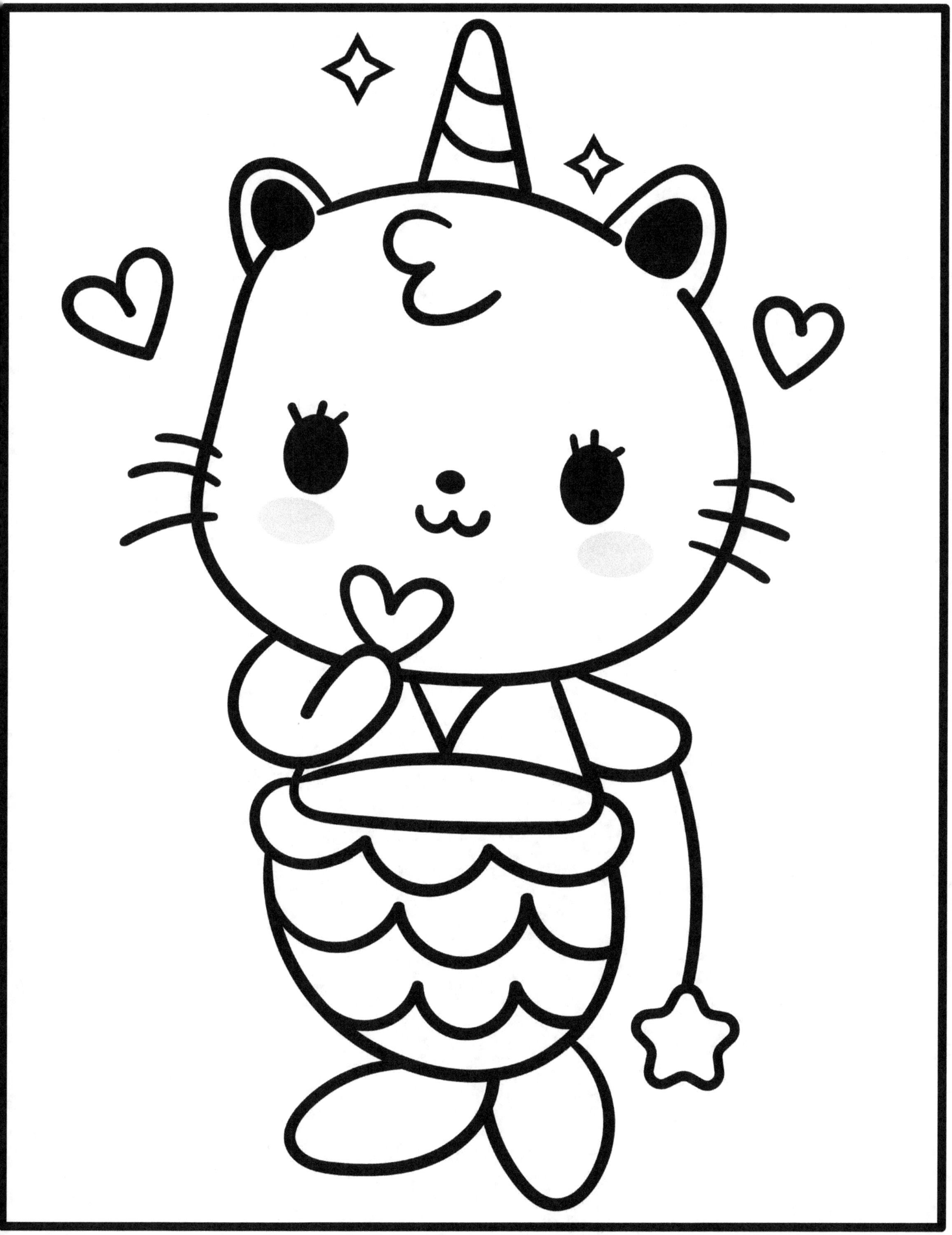

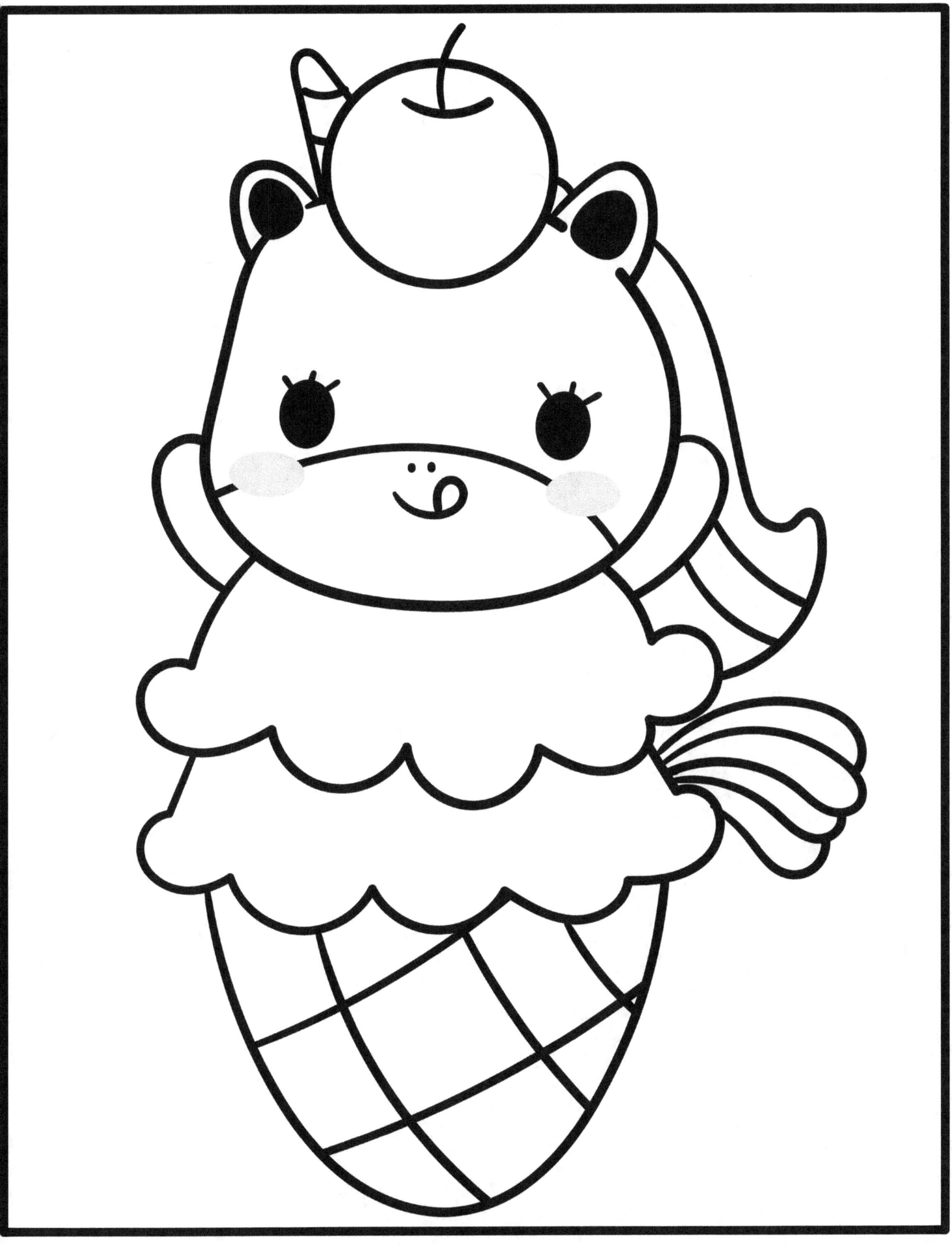

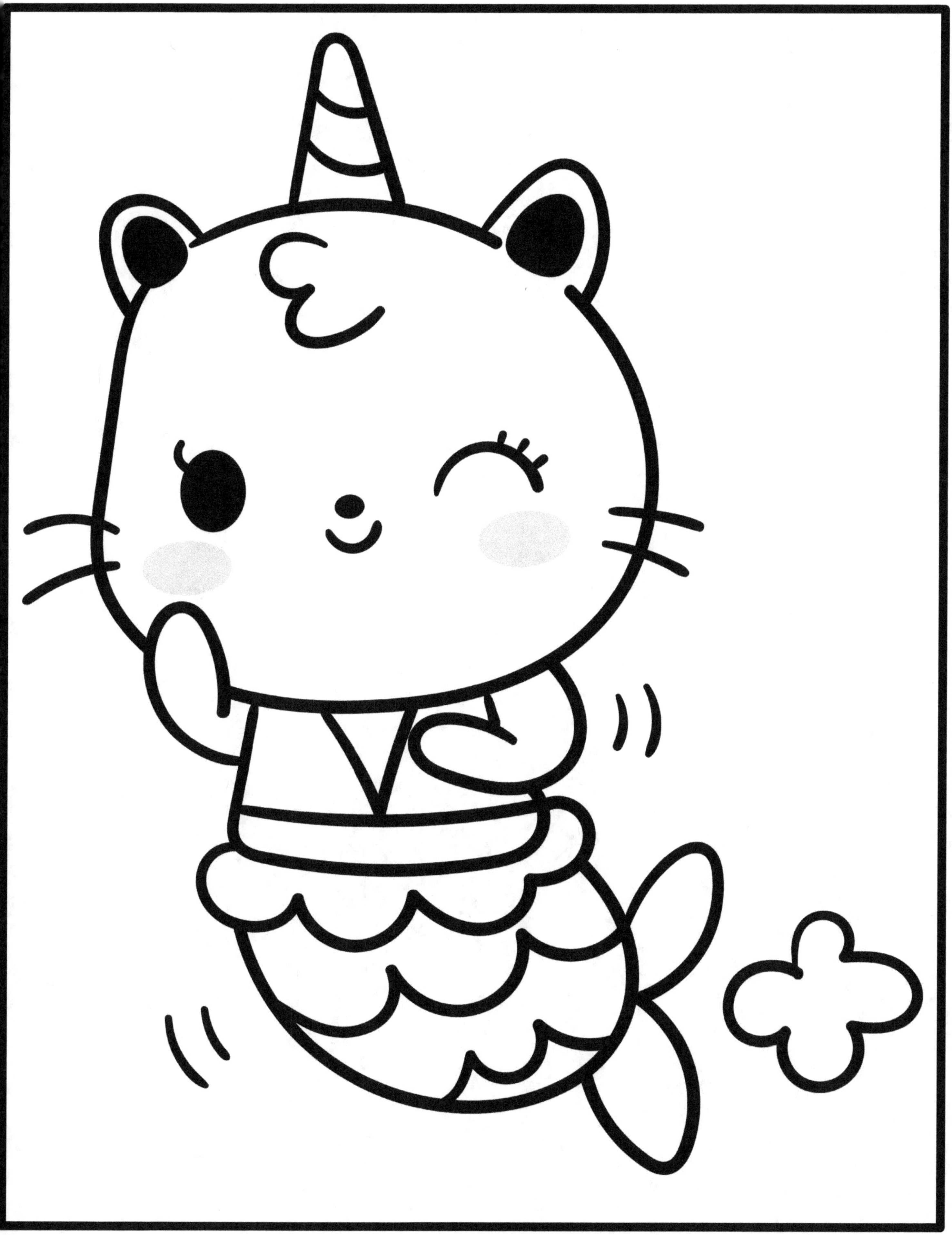

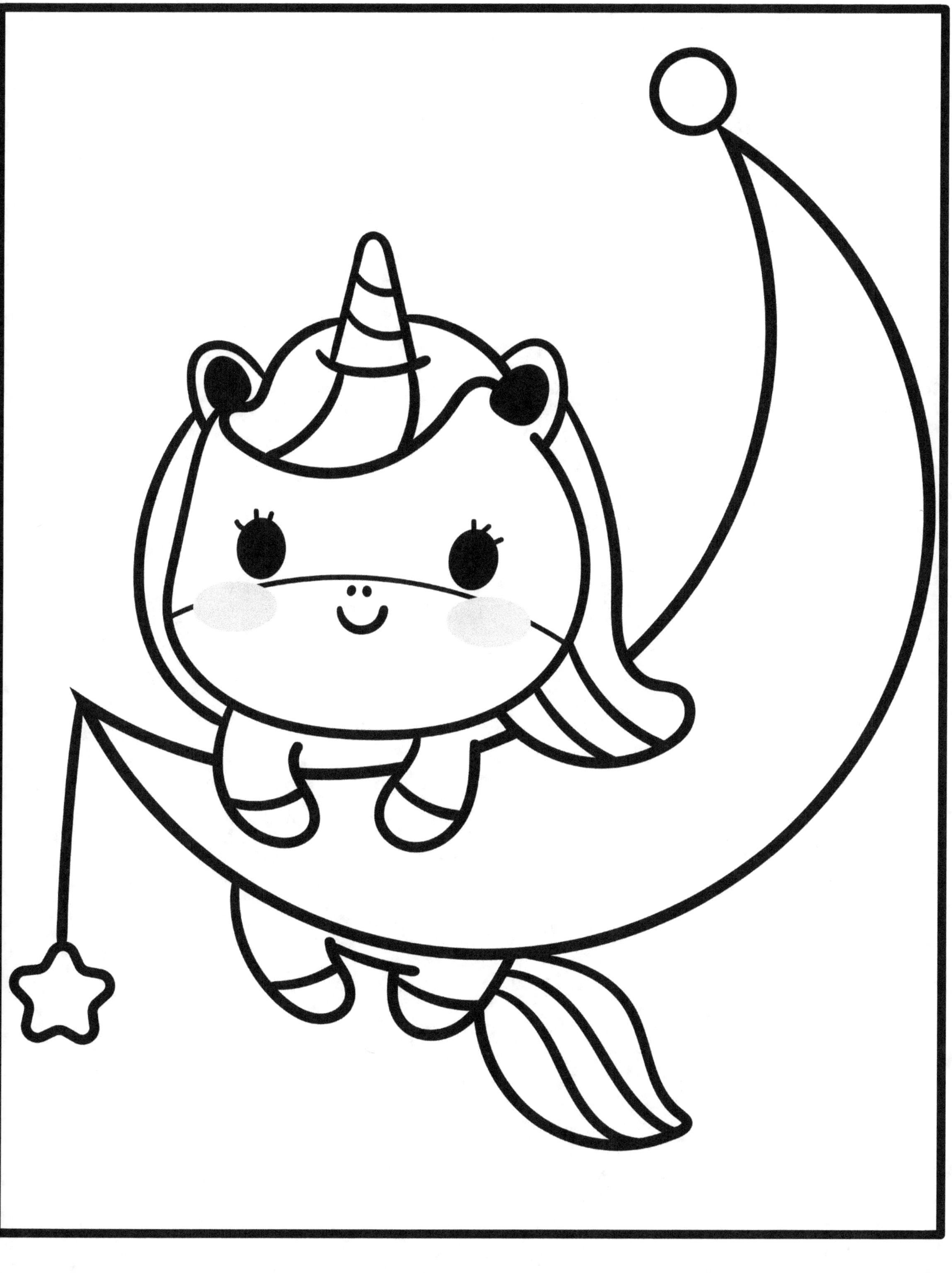

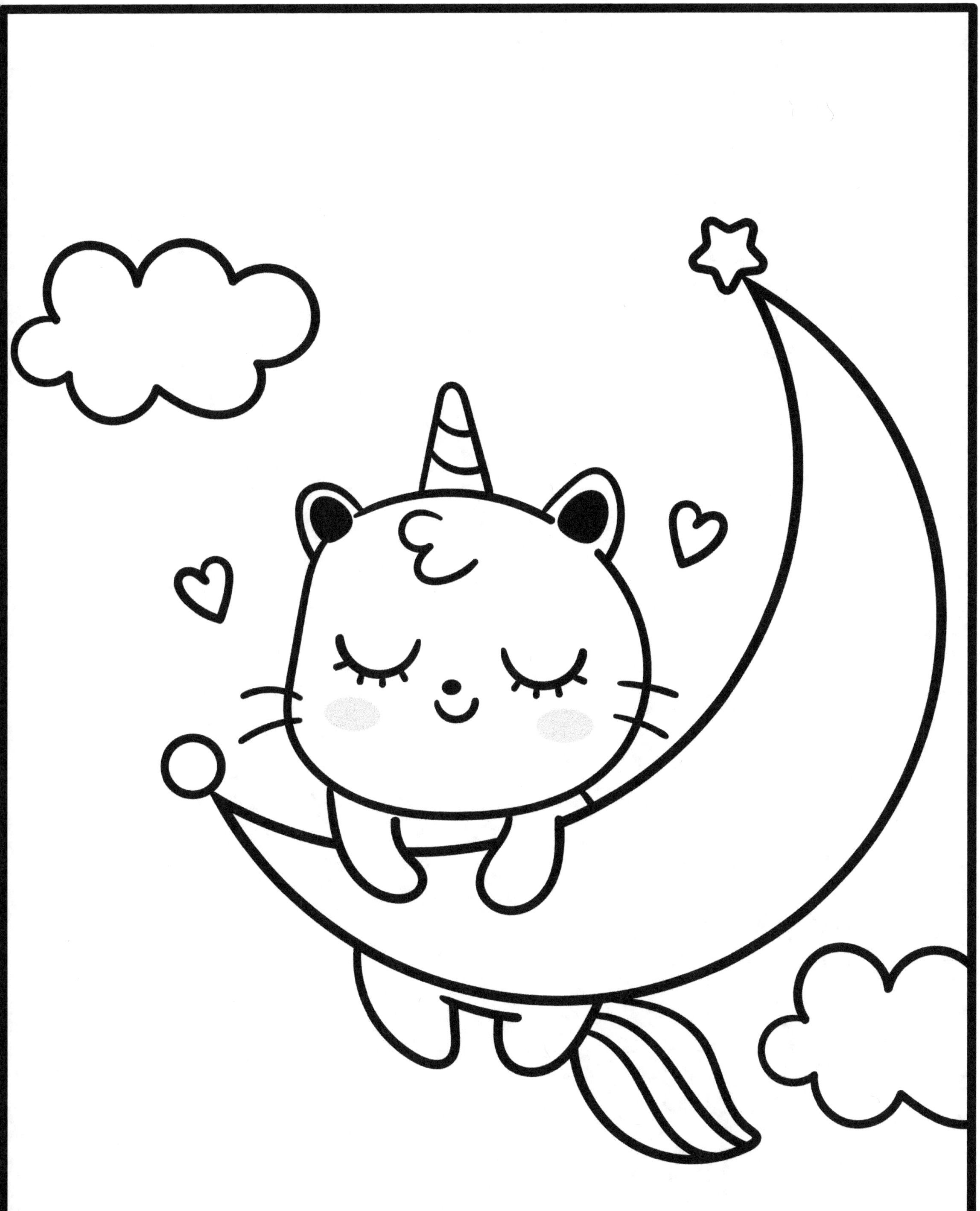

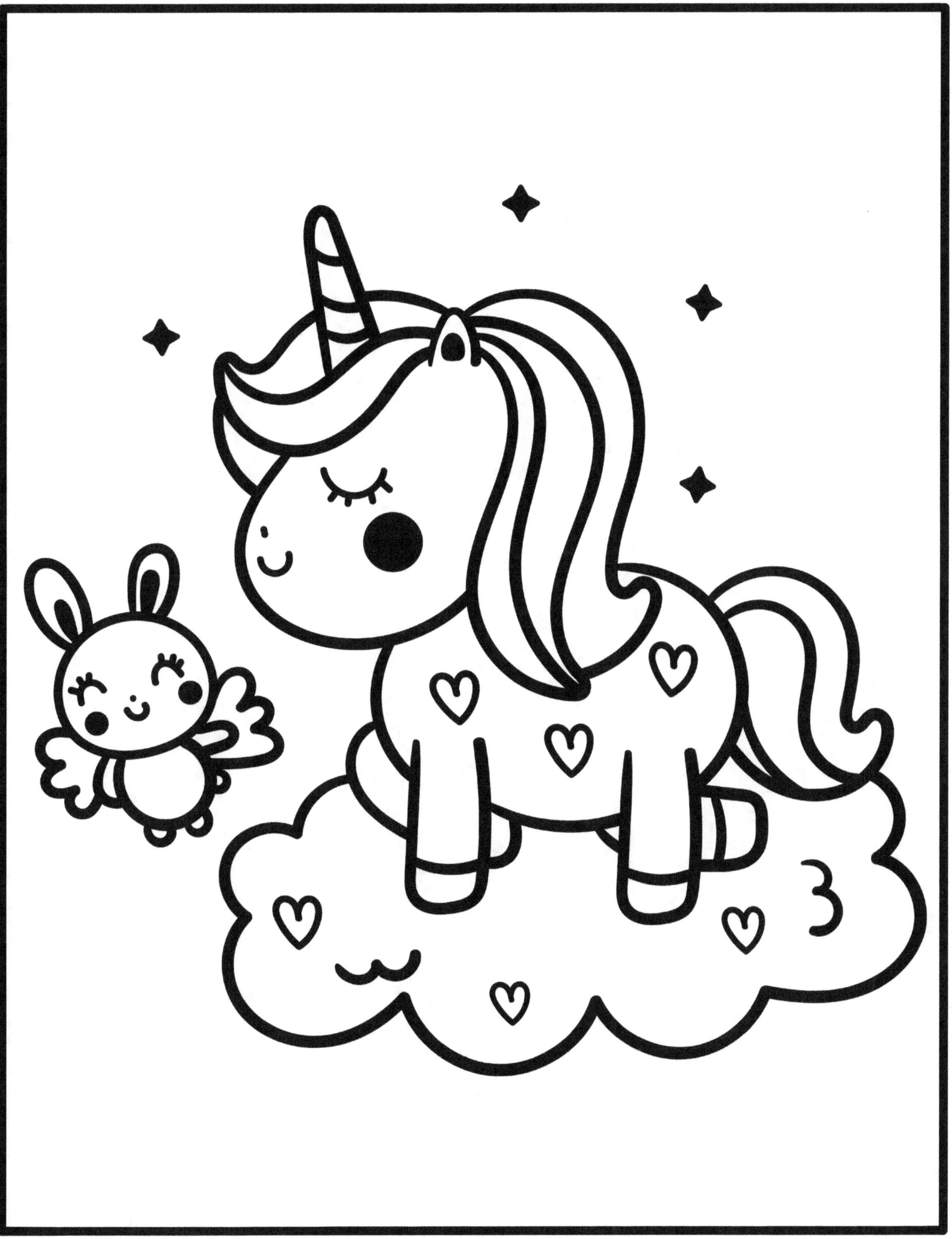

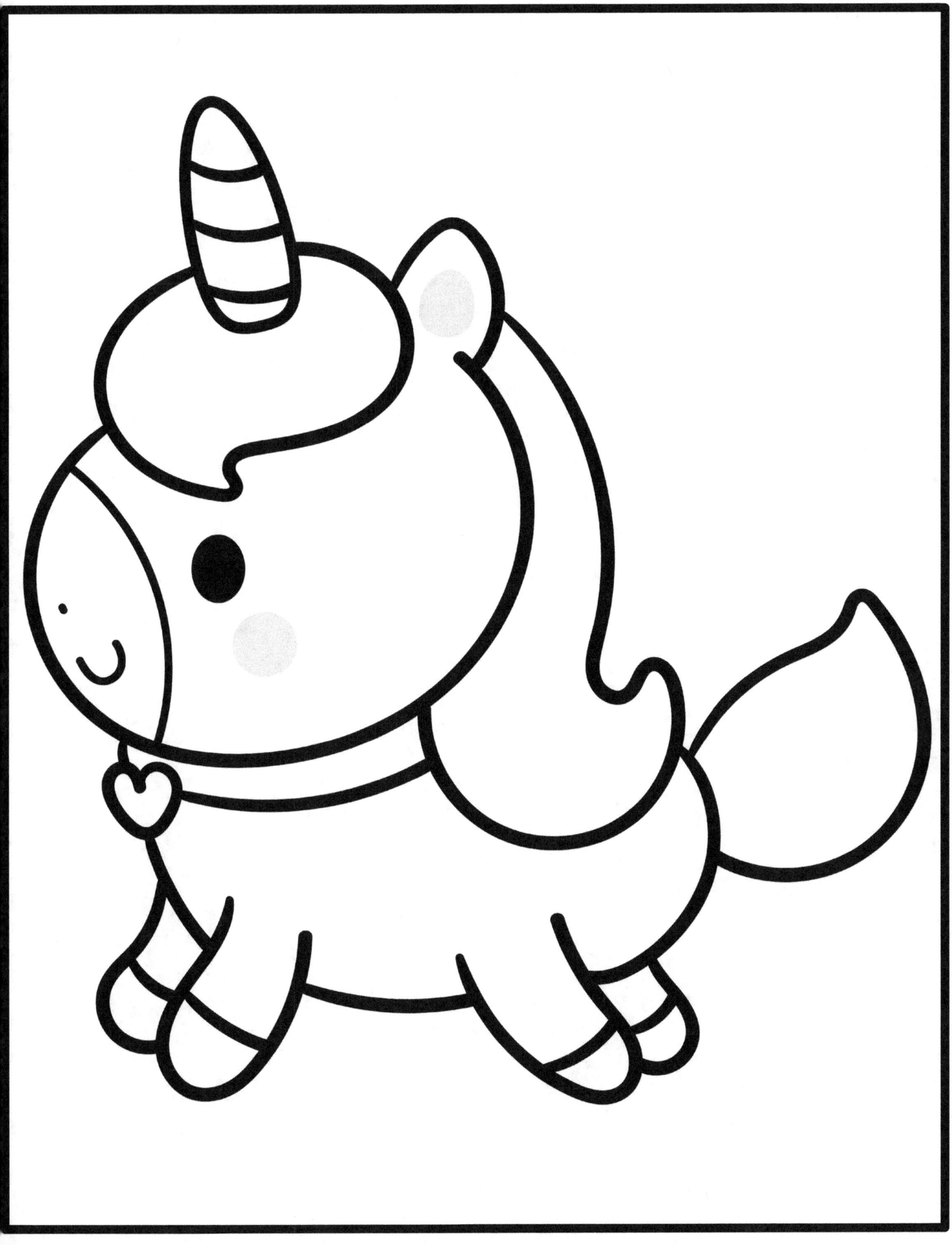

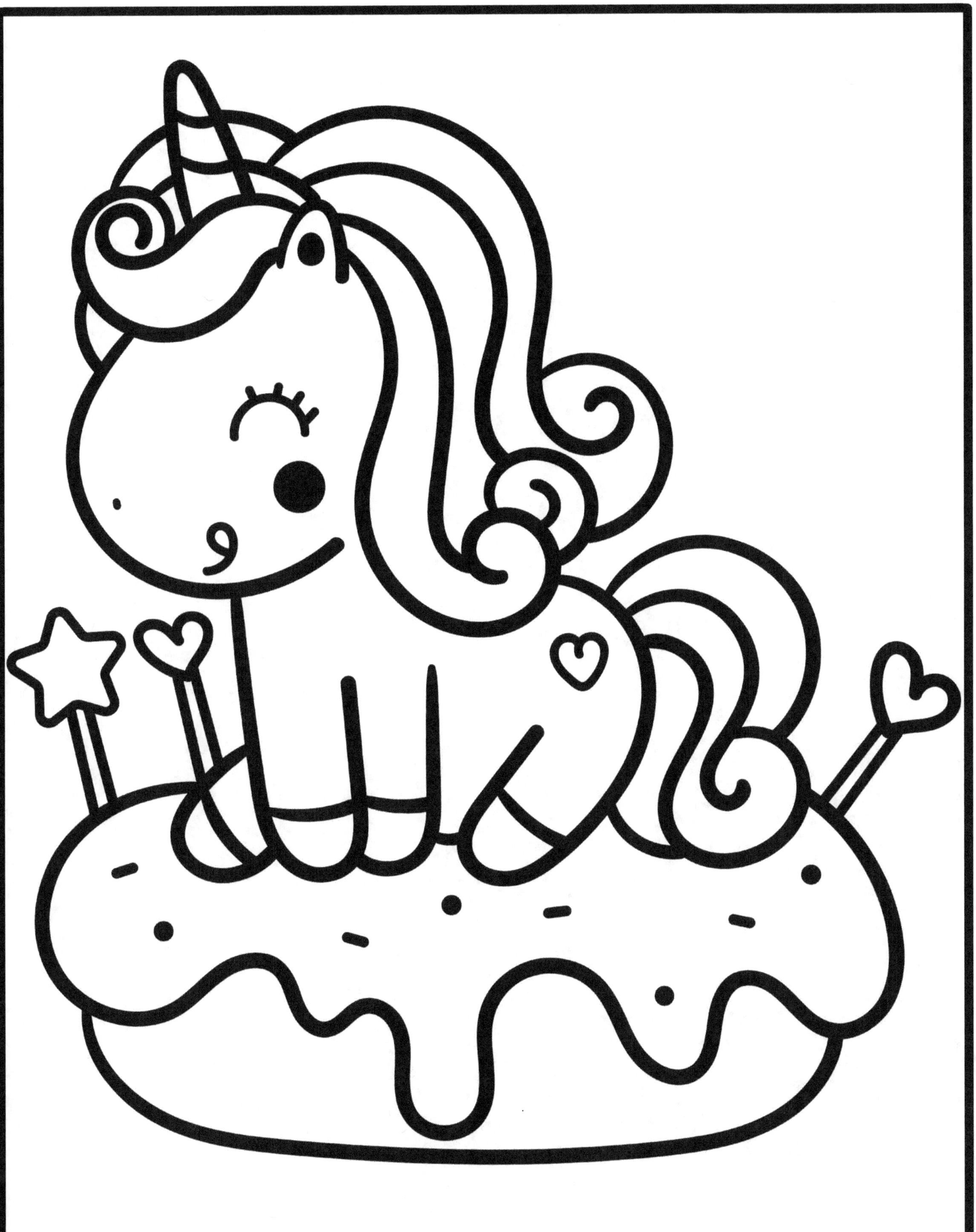

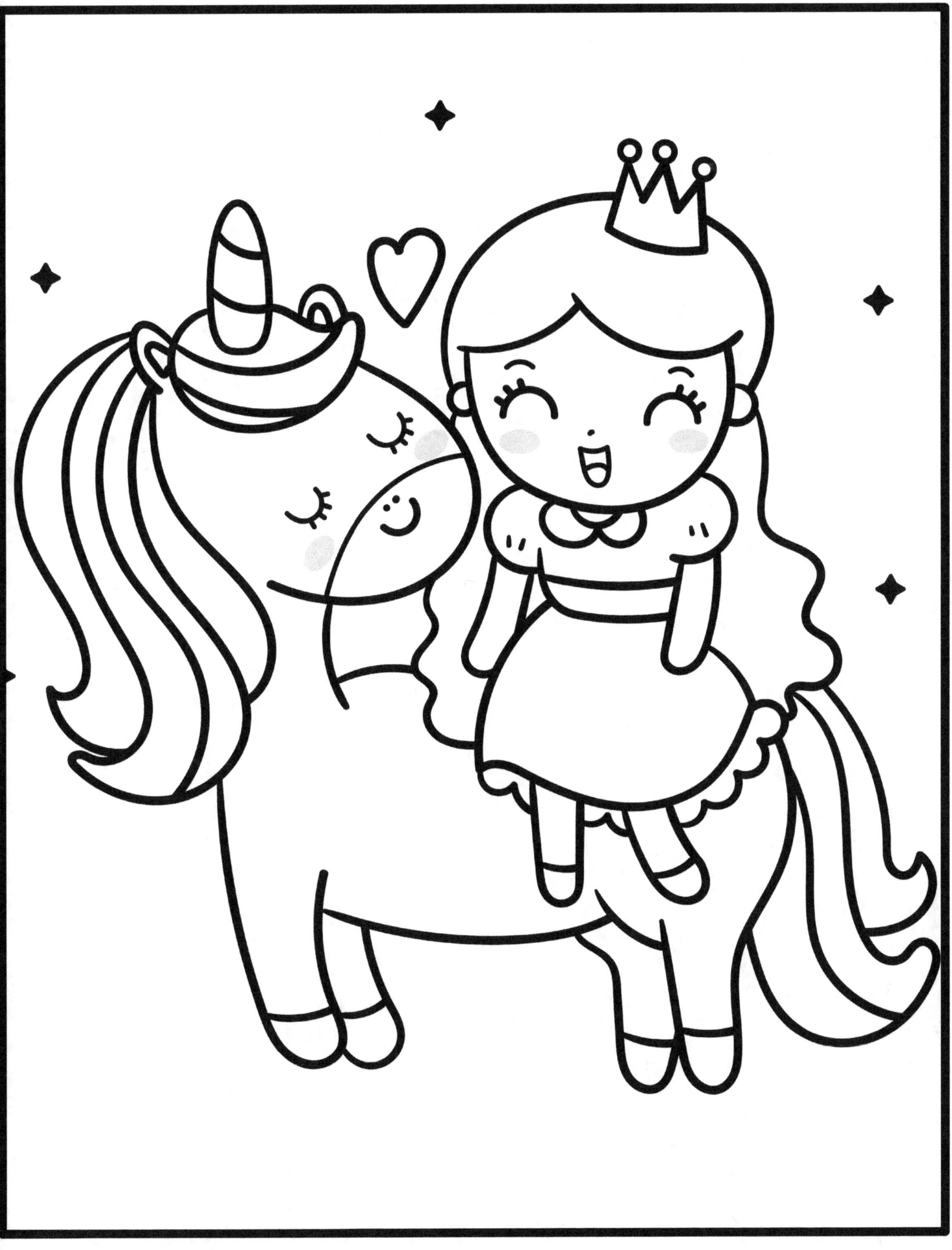

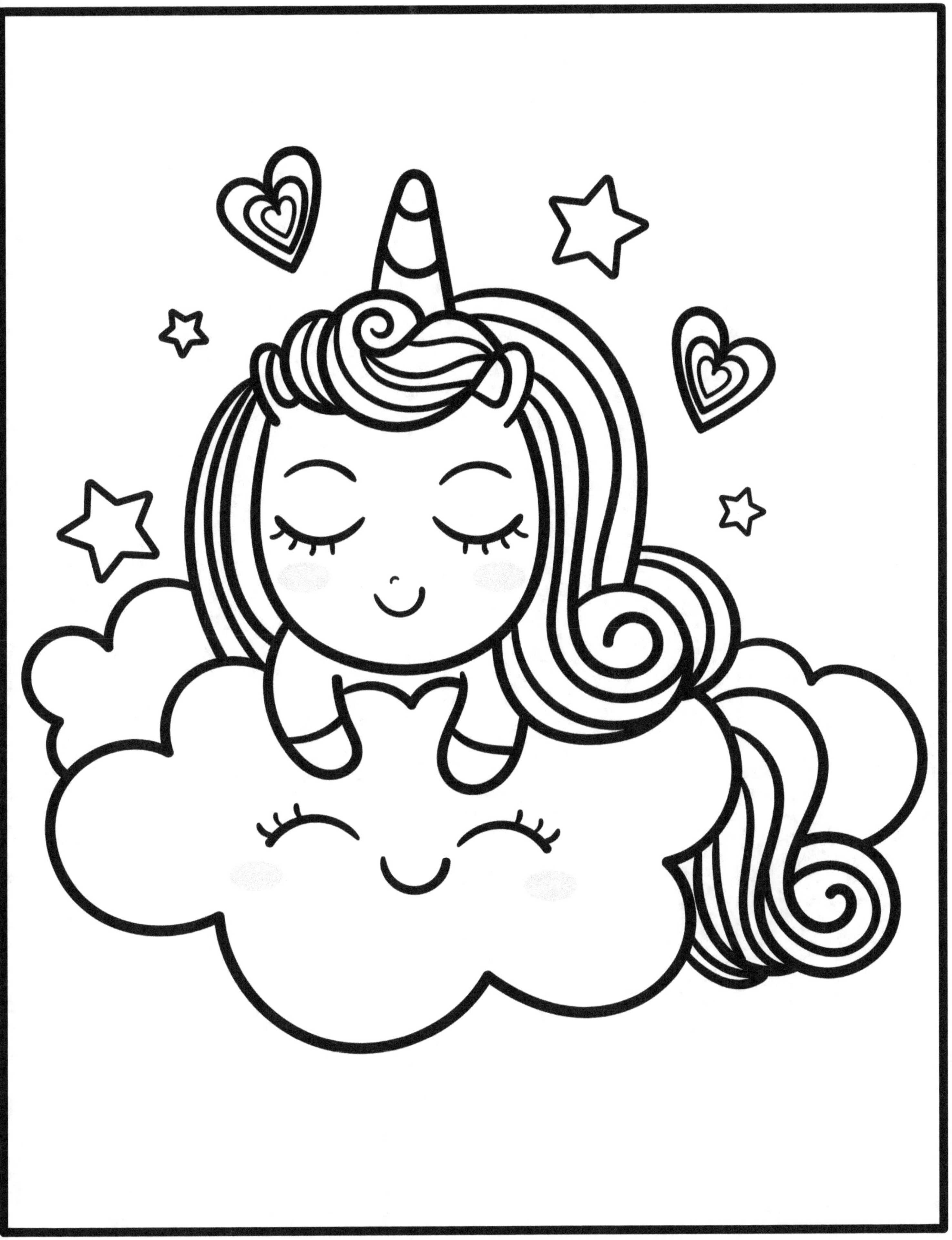

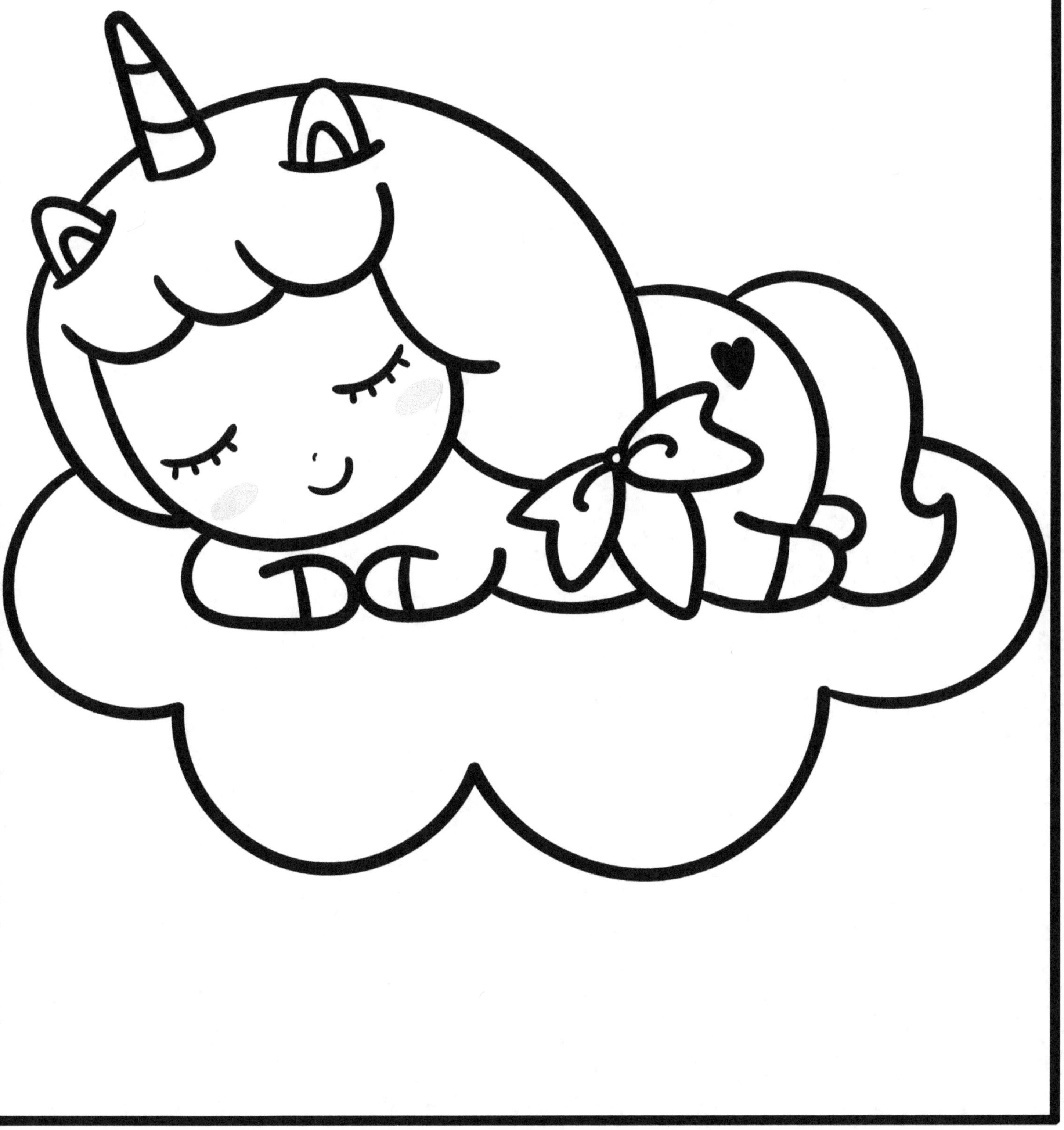

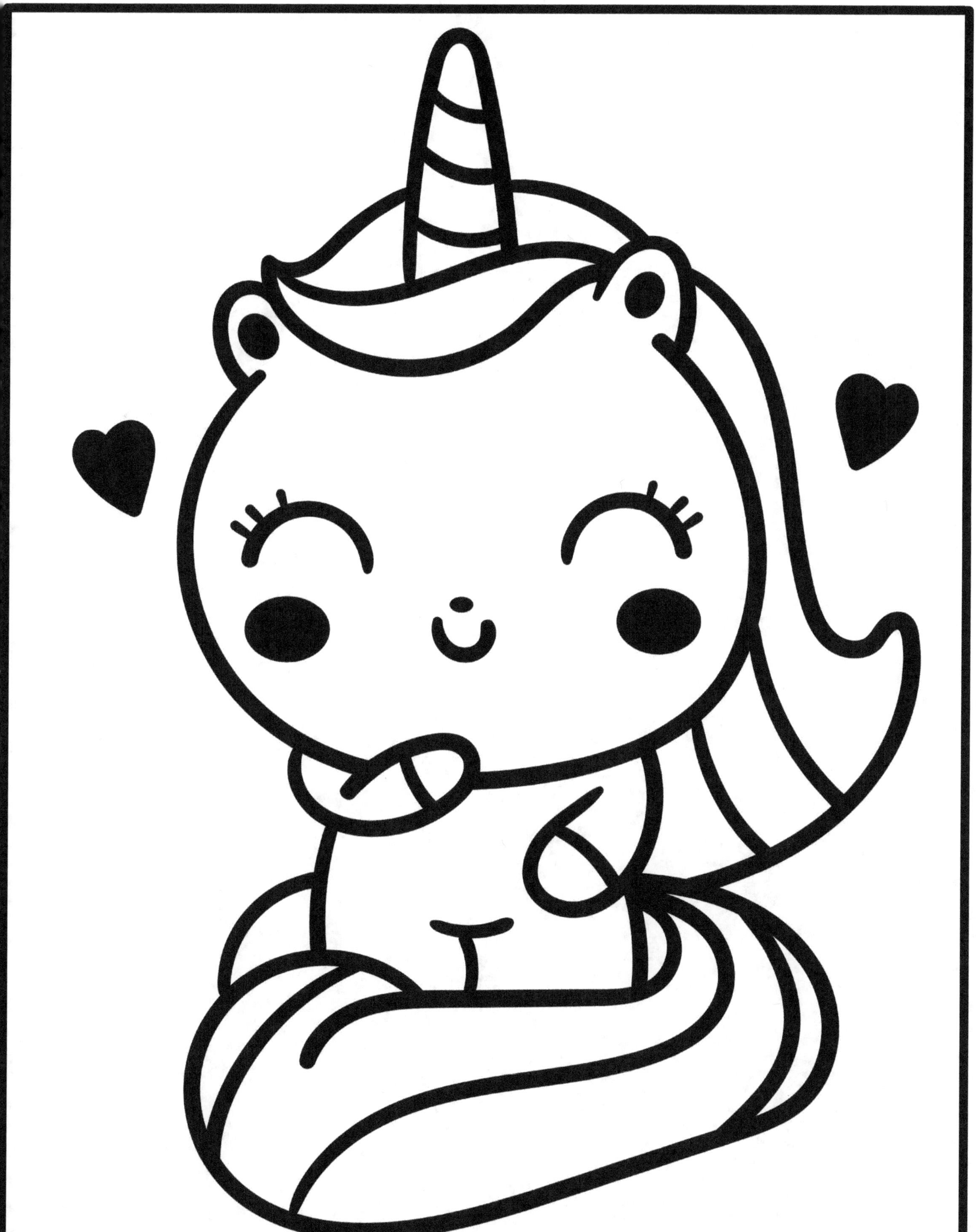

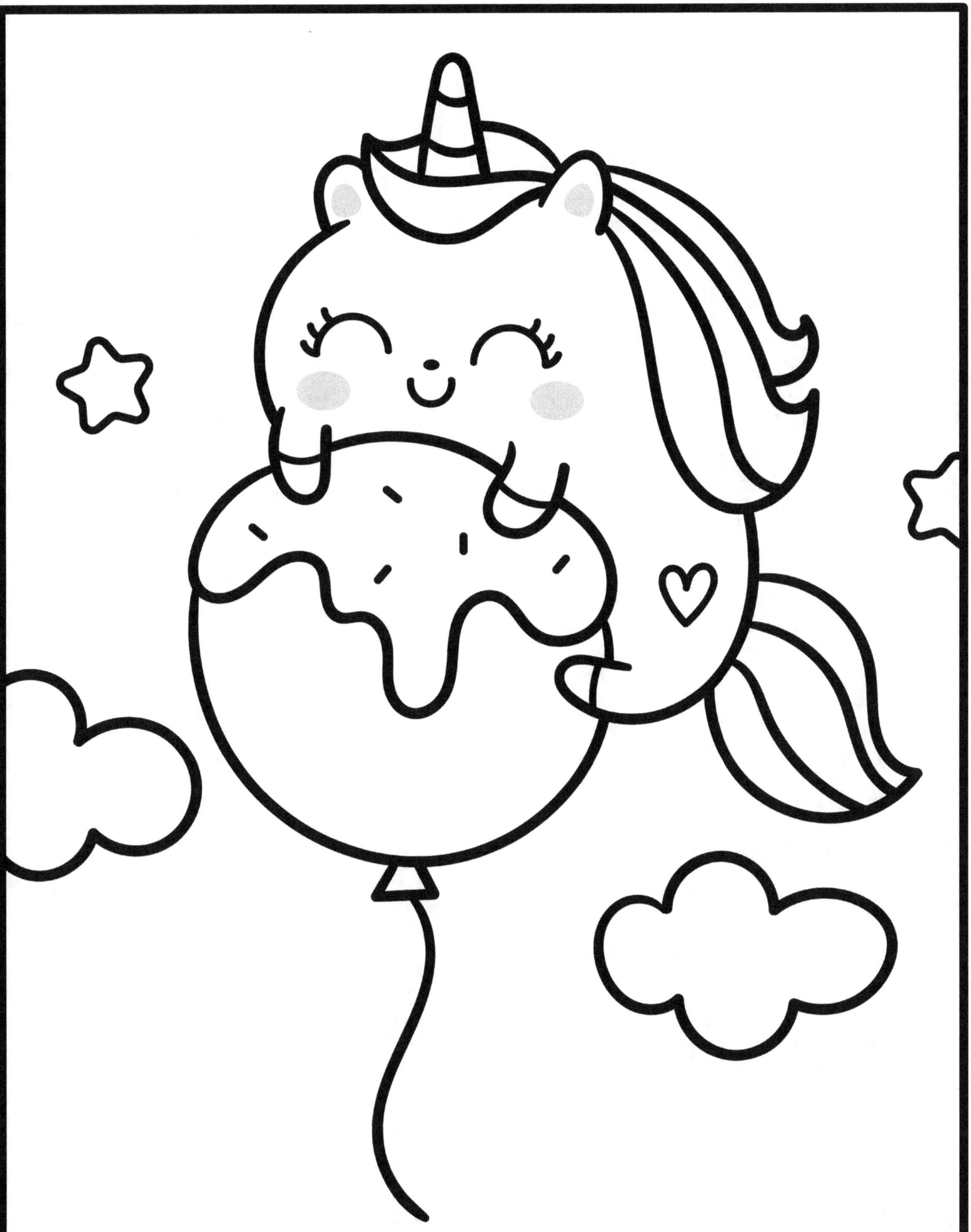

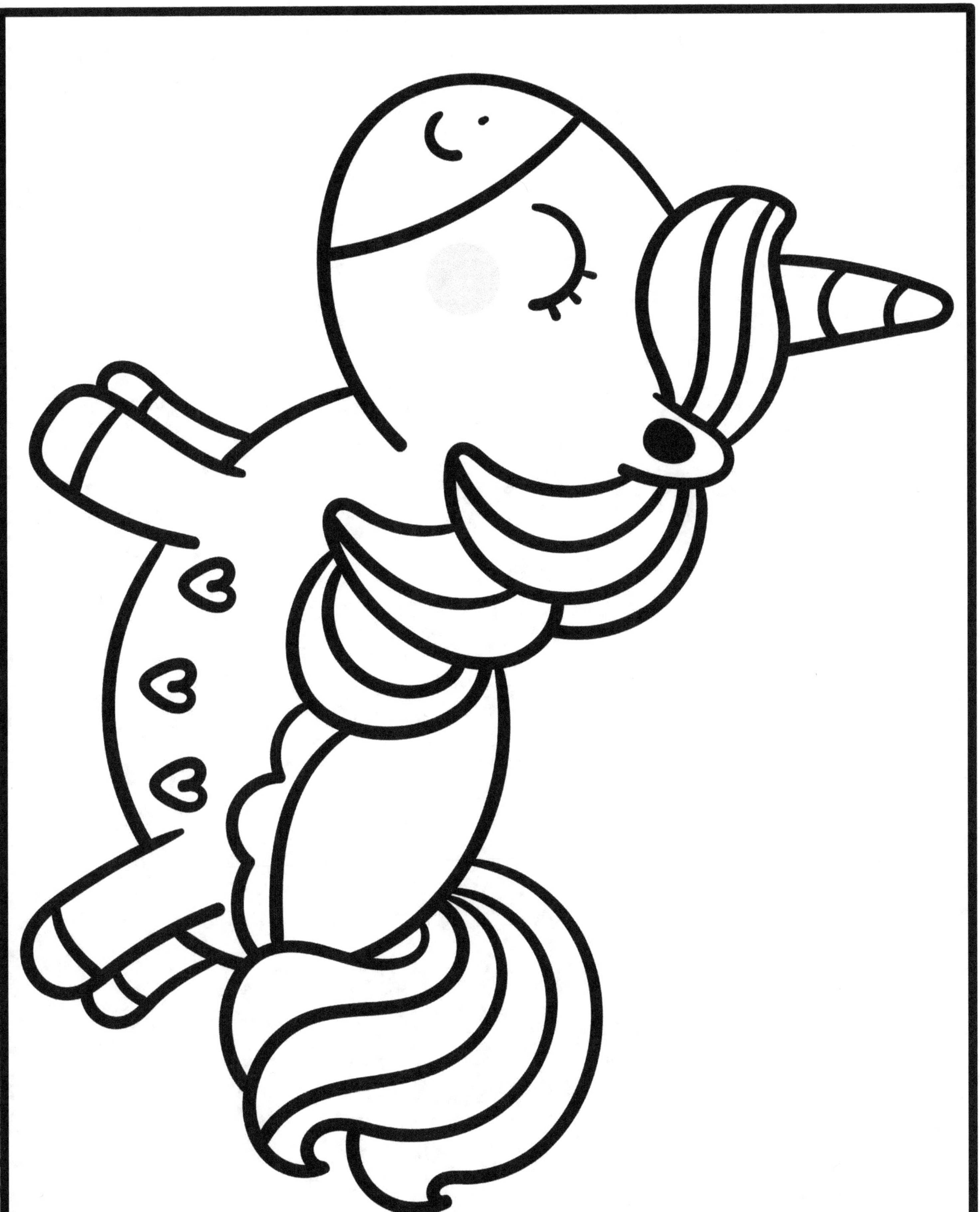

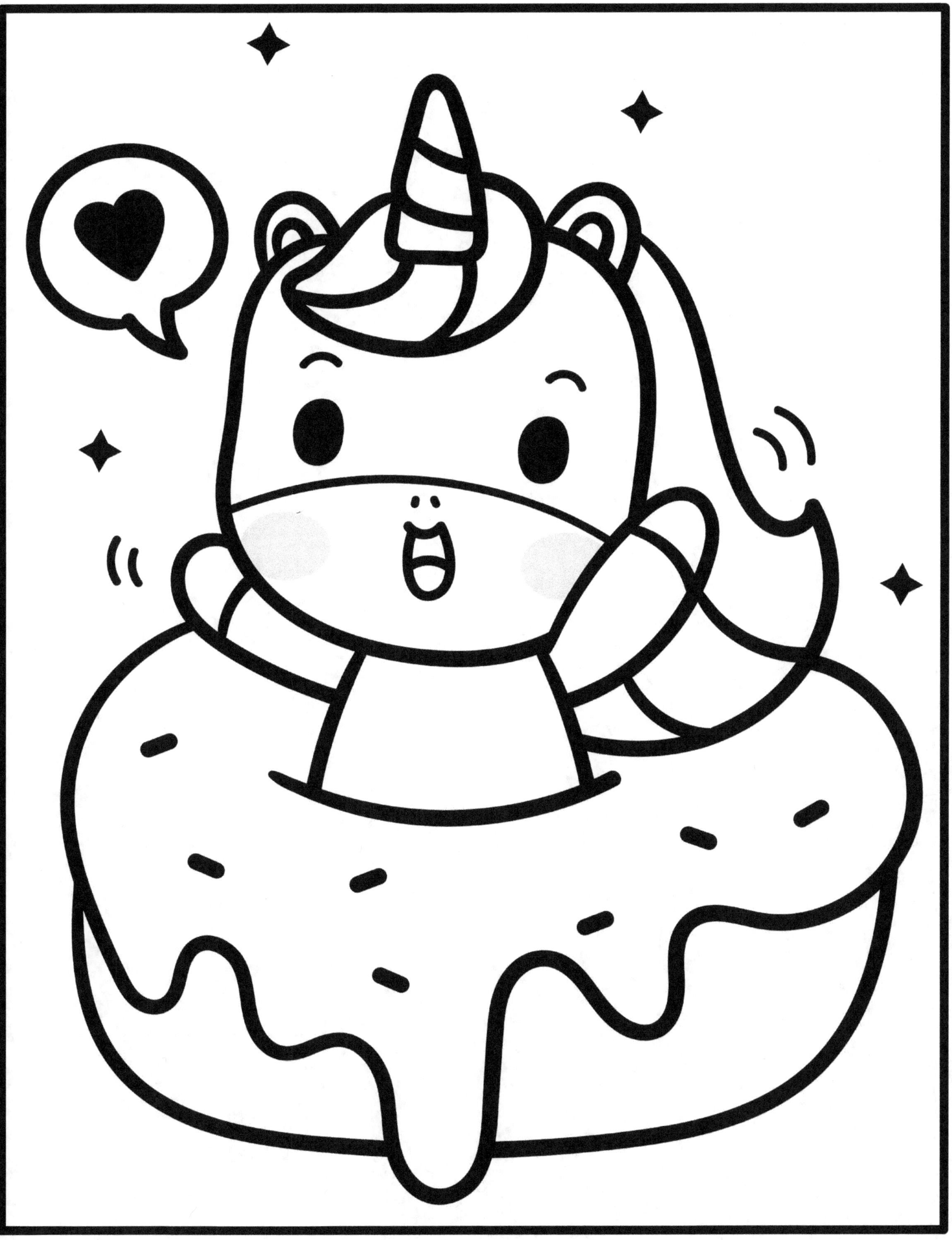

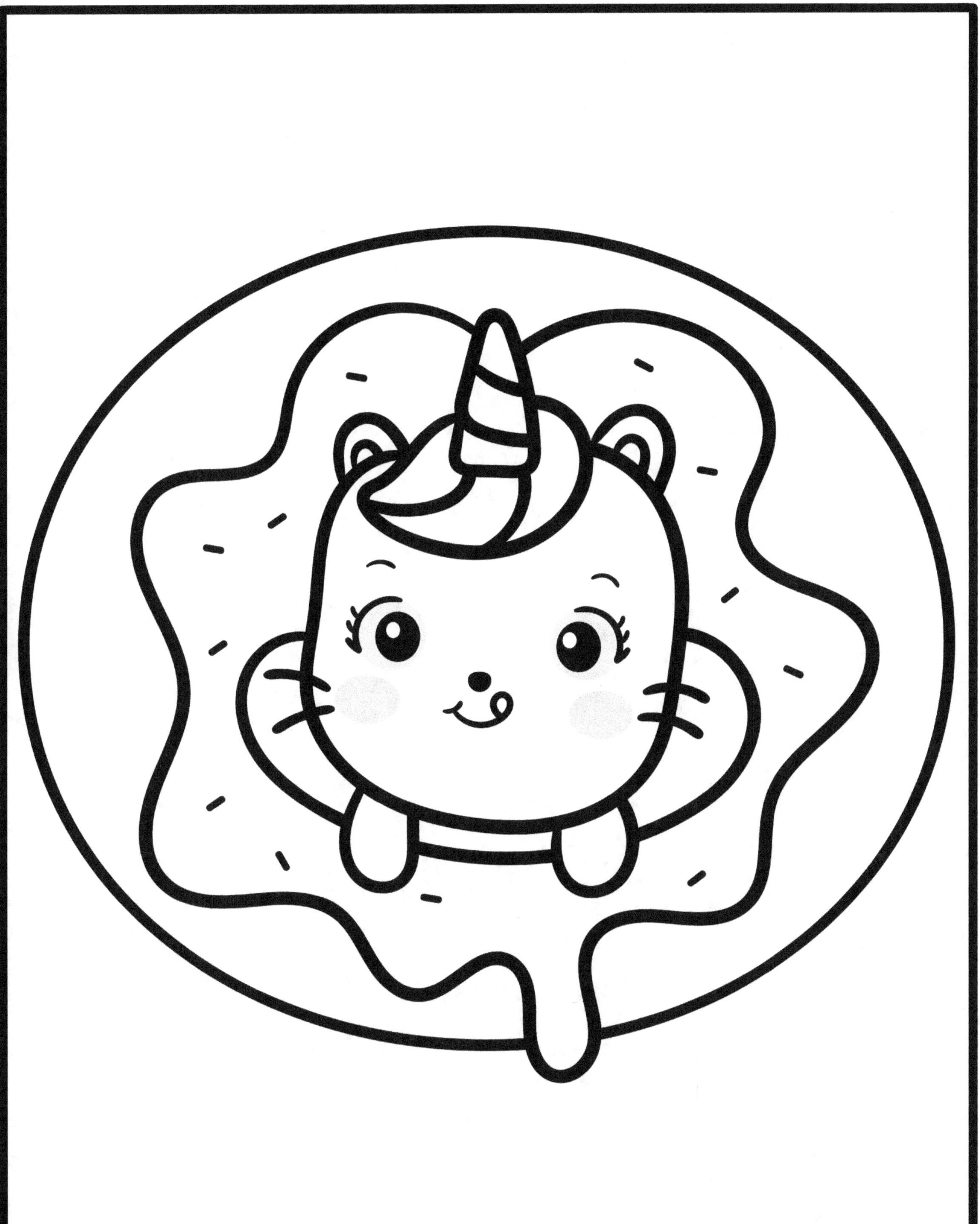

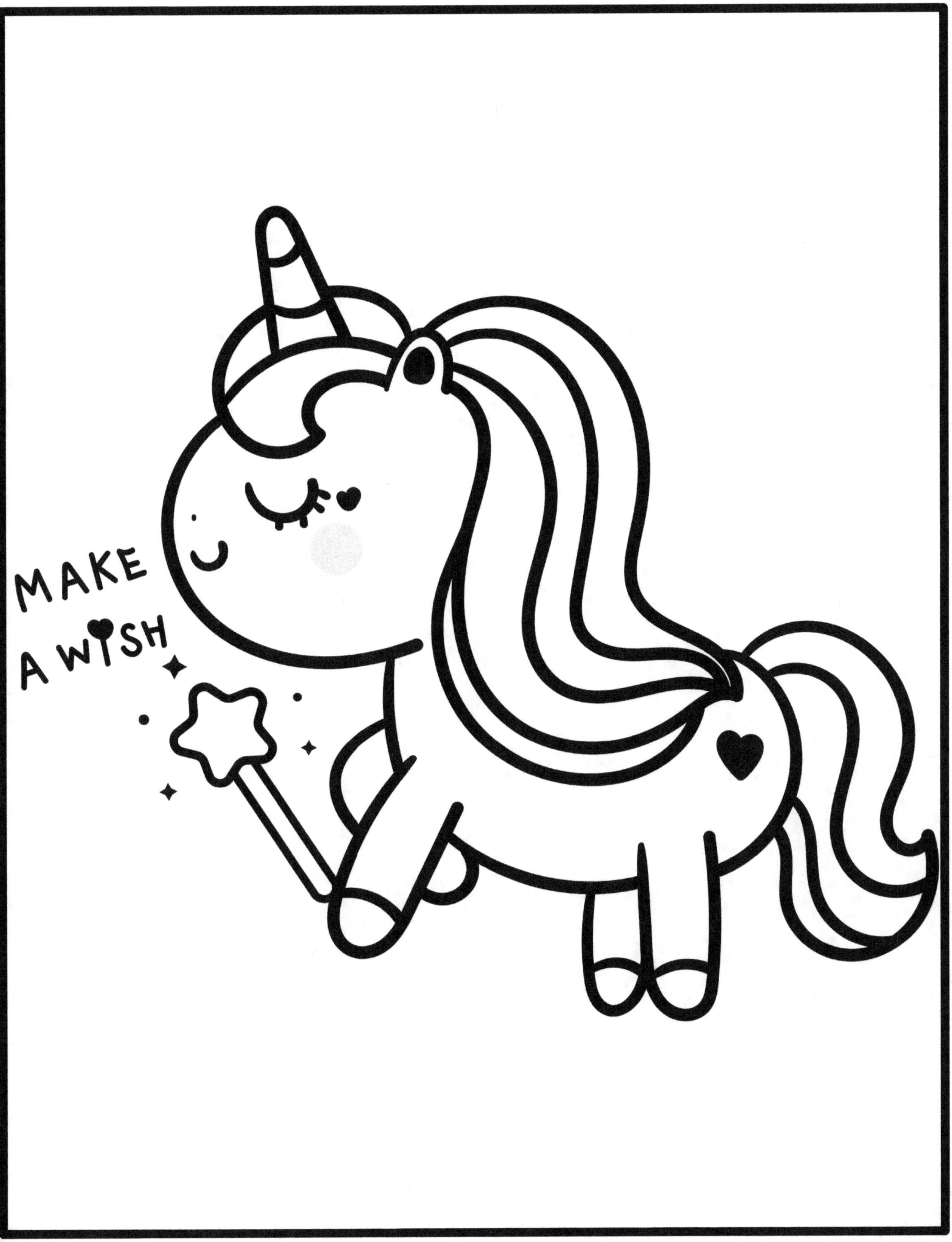
MAKE
A WISH

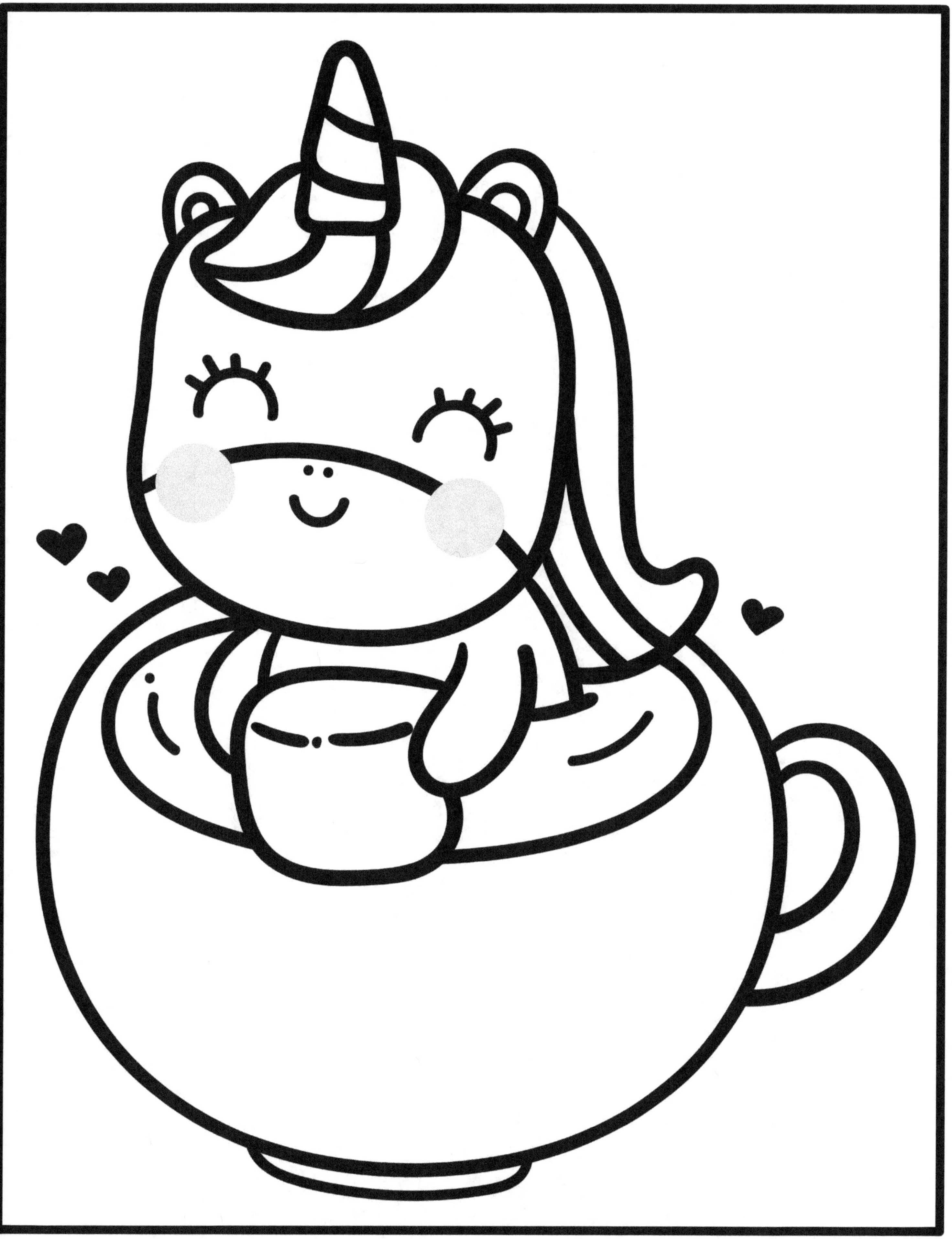

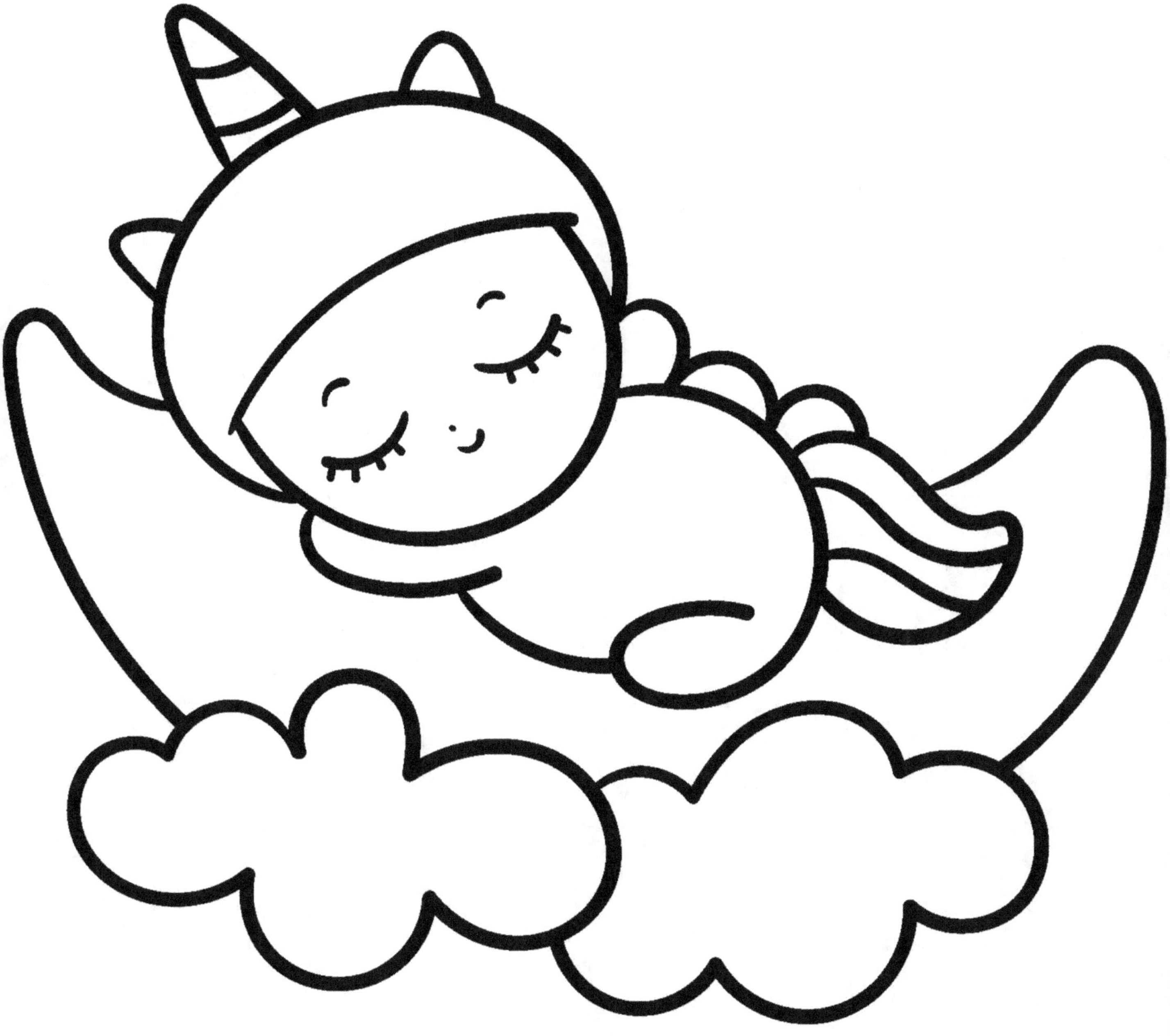

Sweet Dream

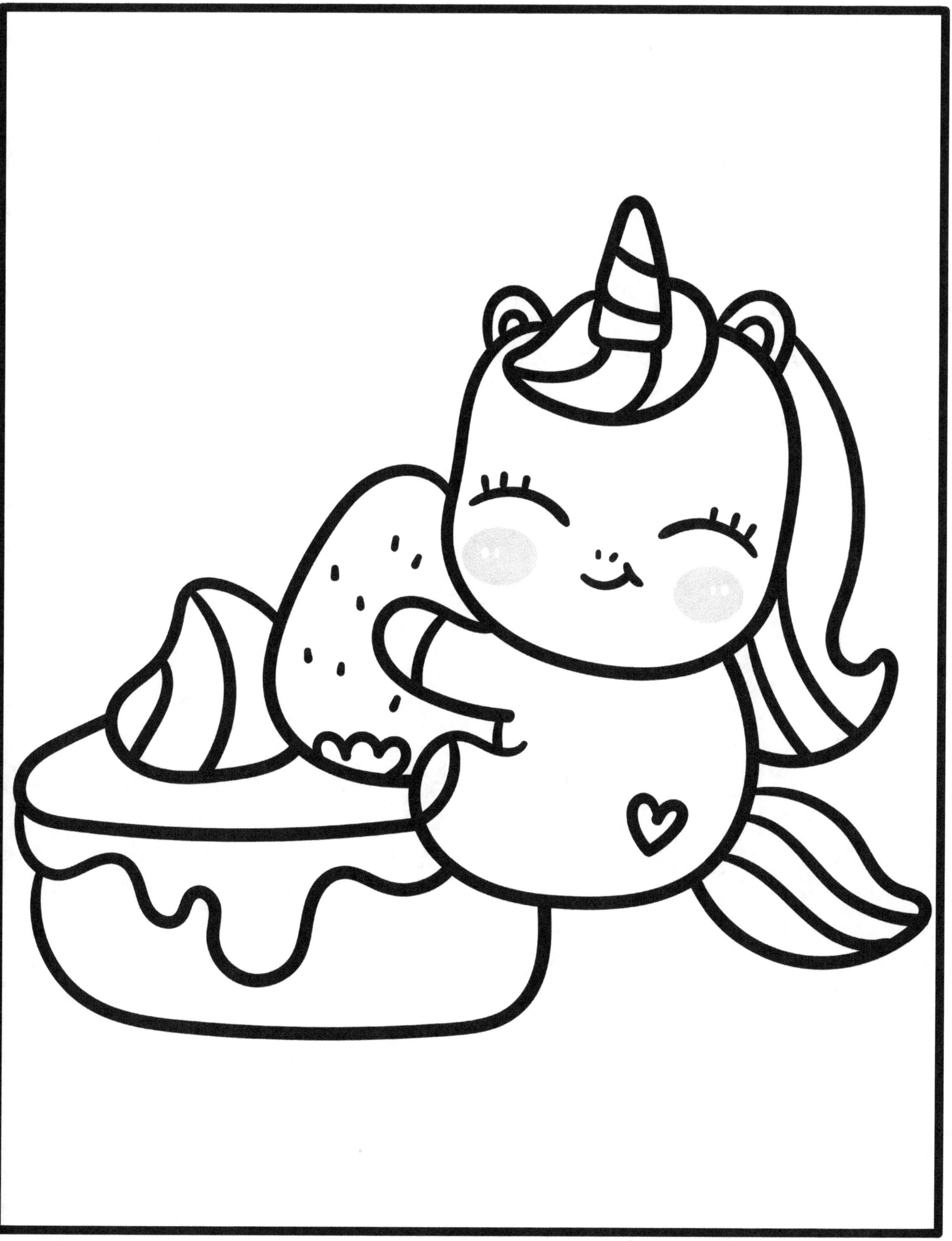

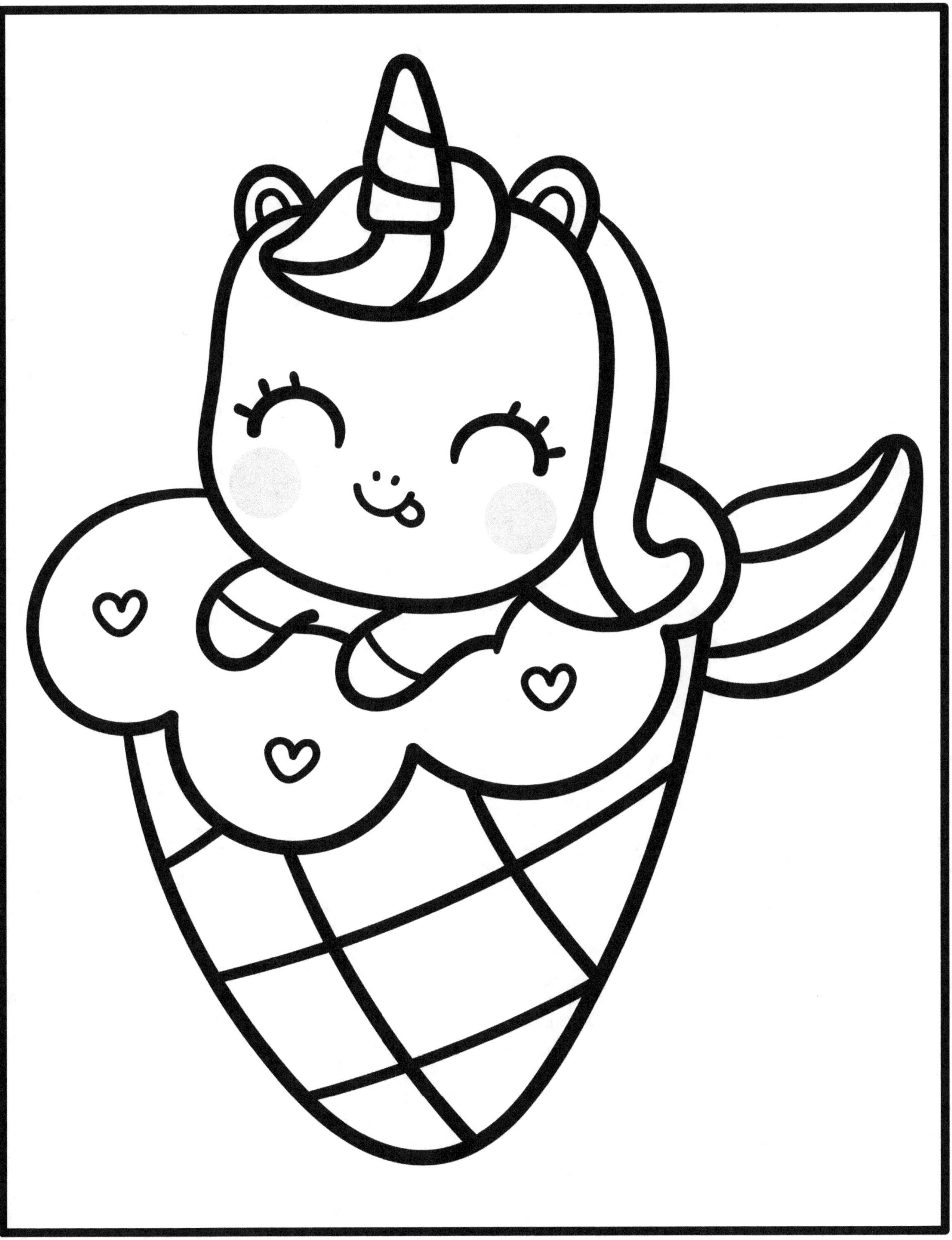

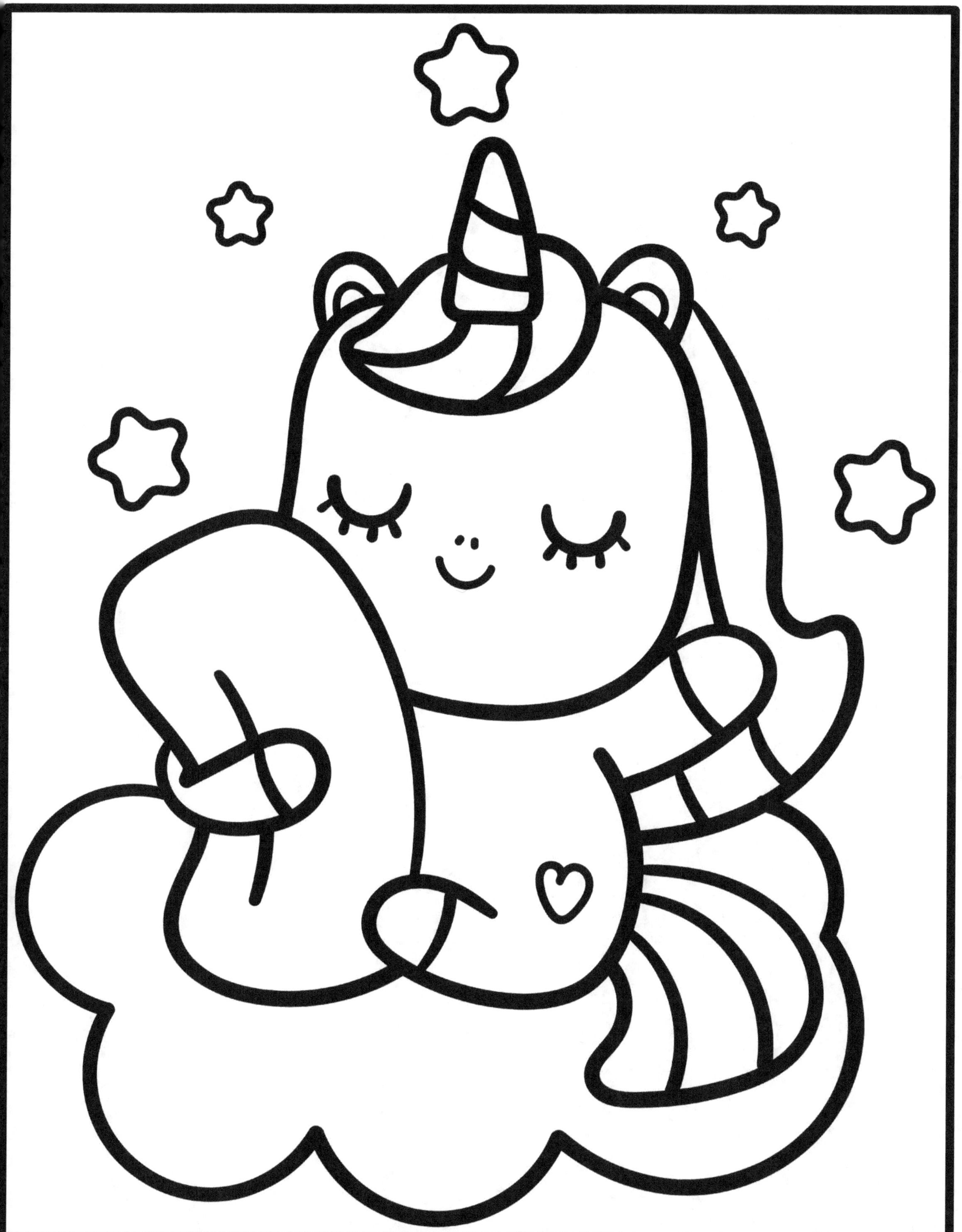

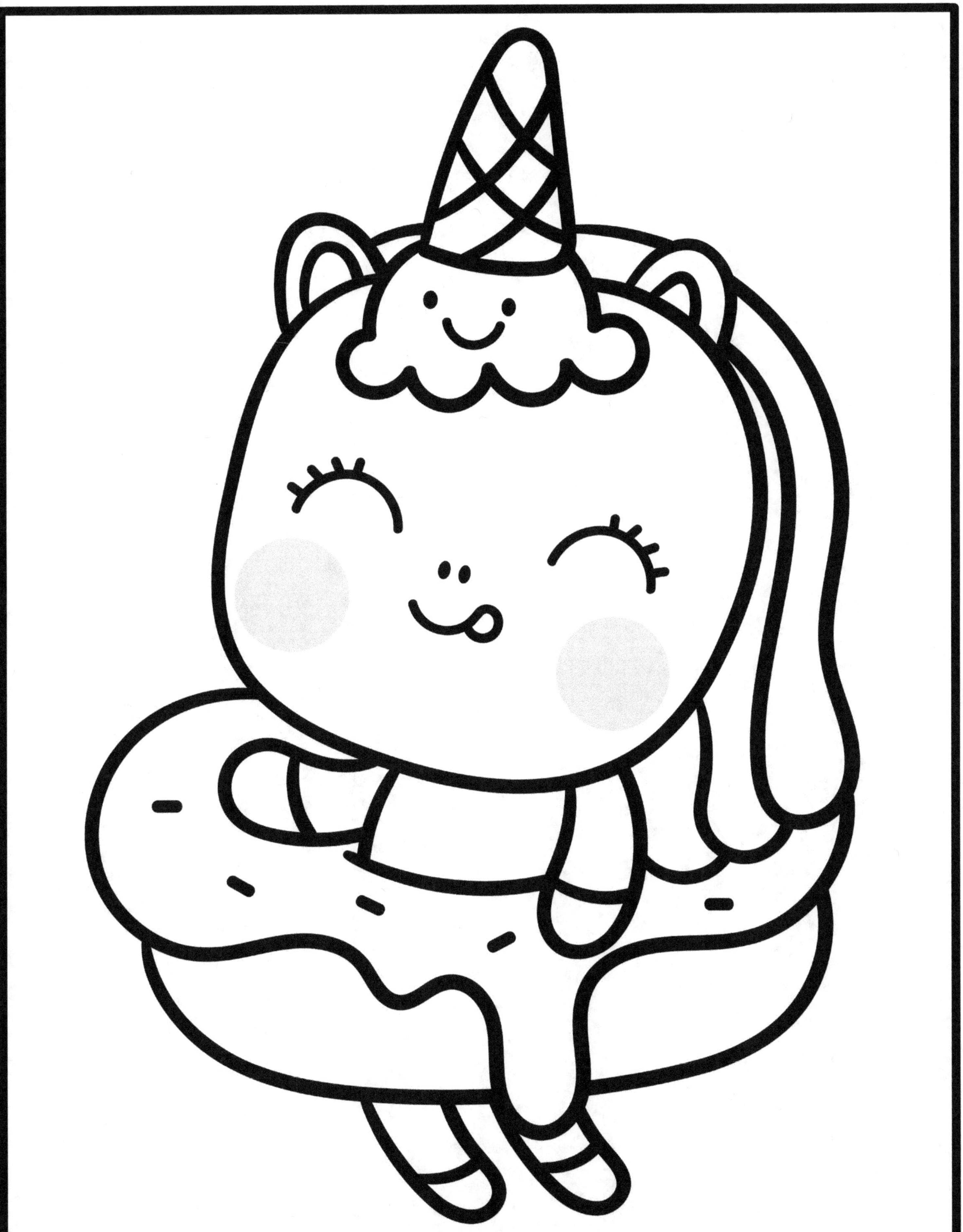

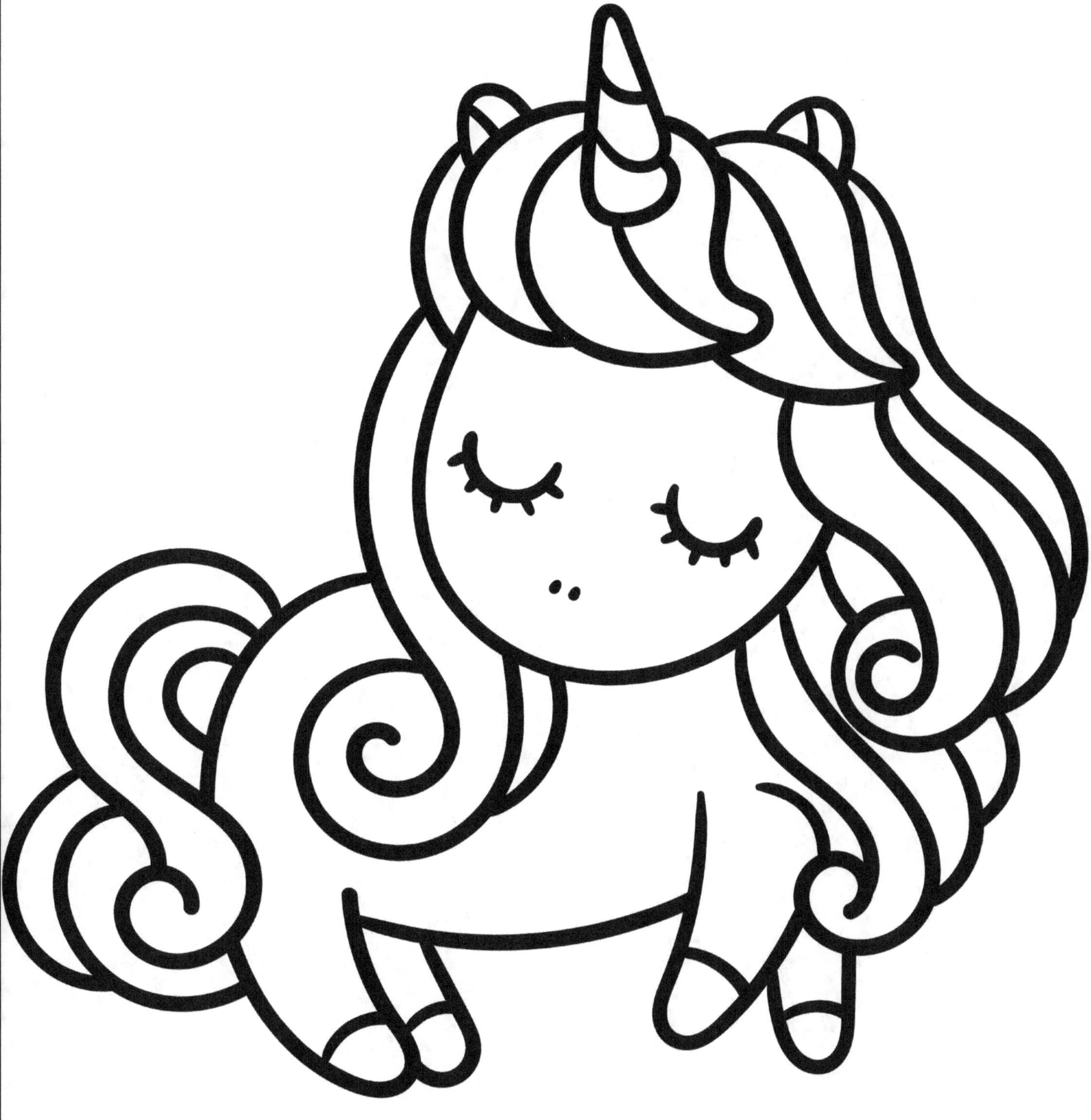

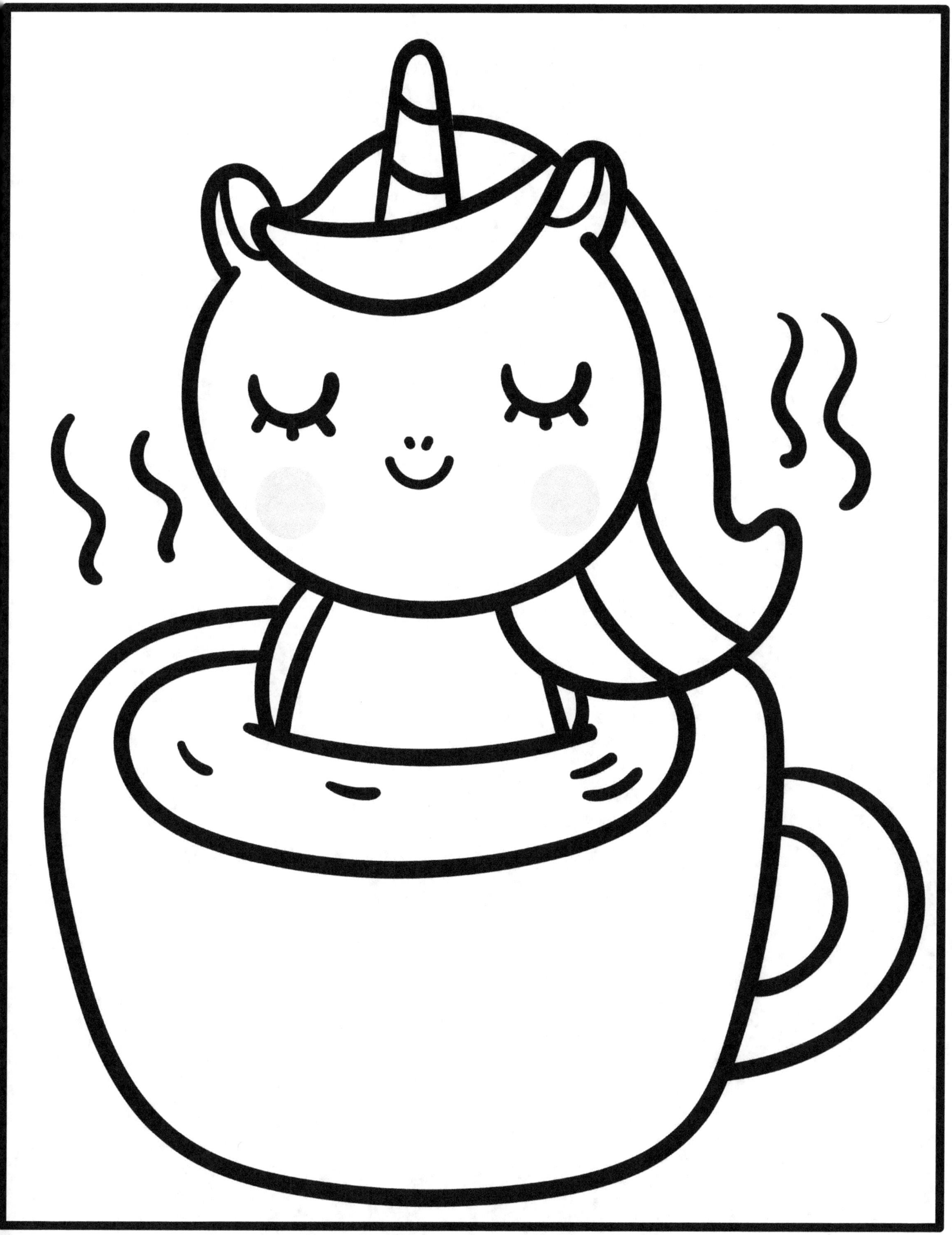

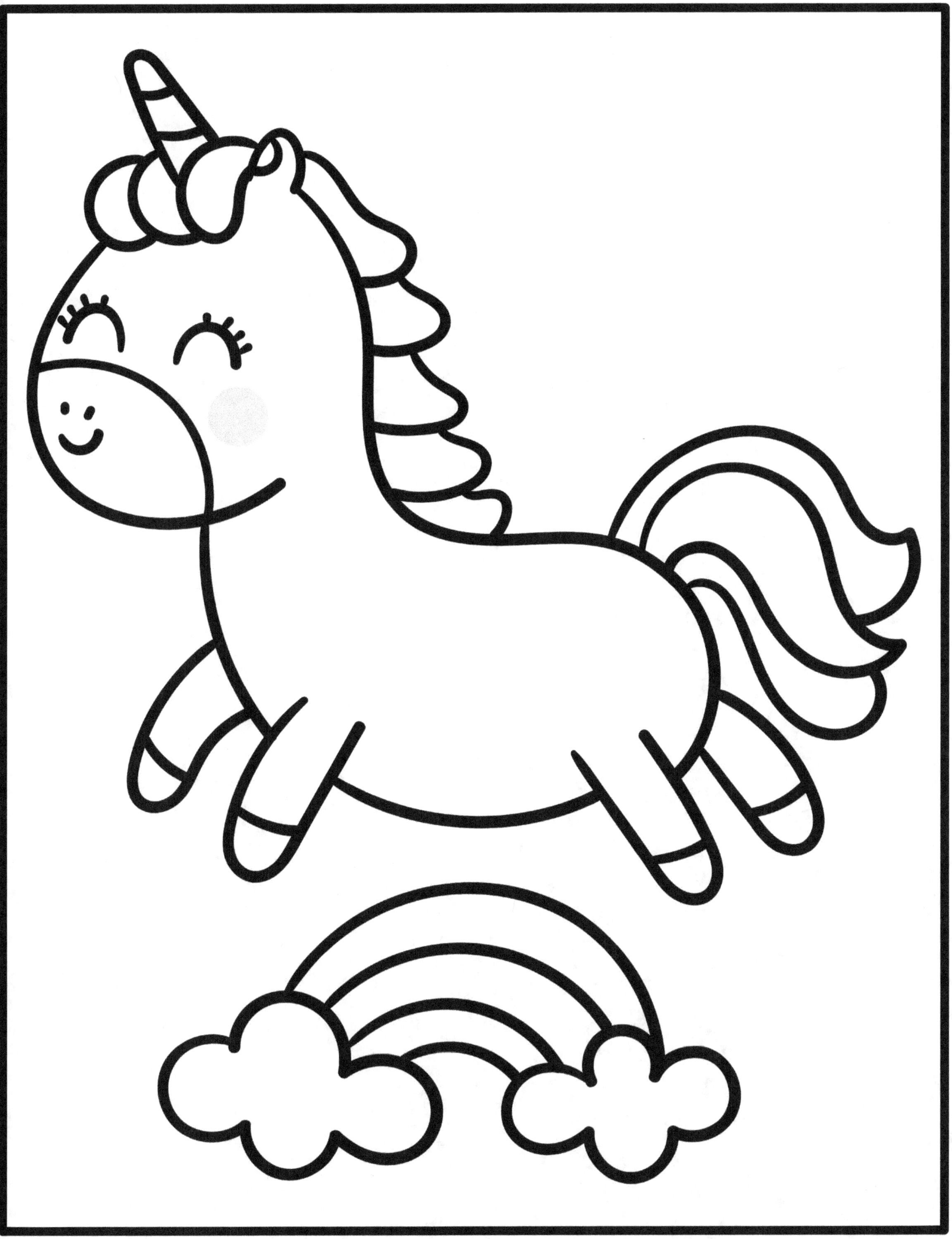

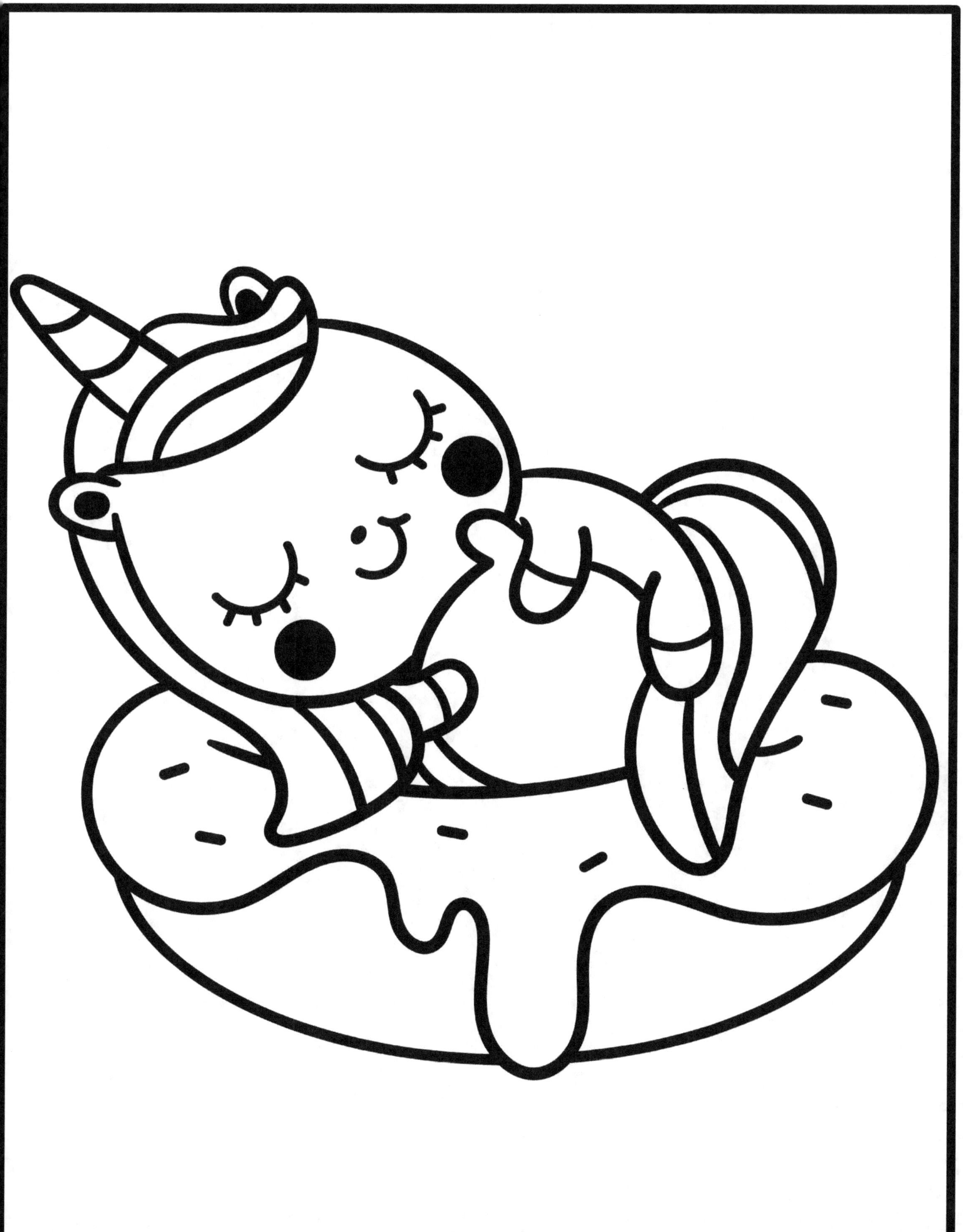

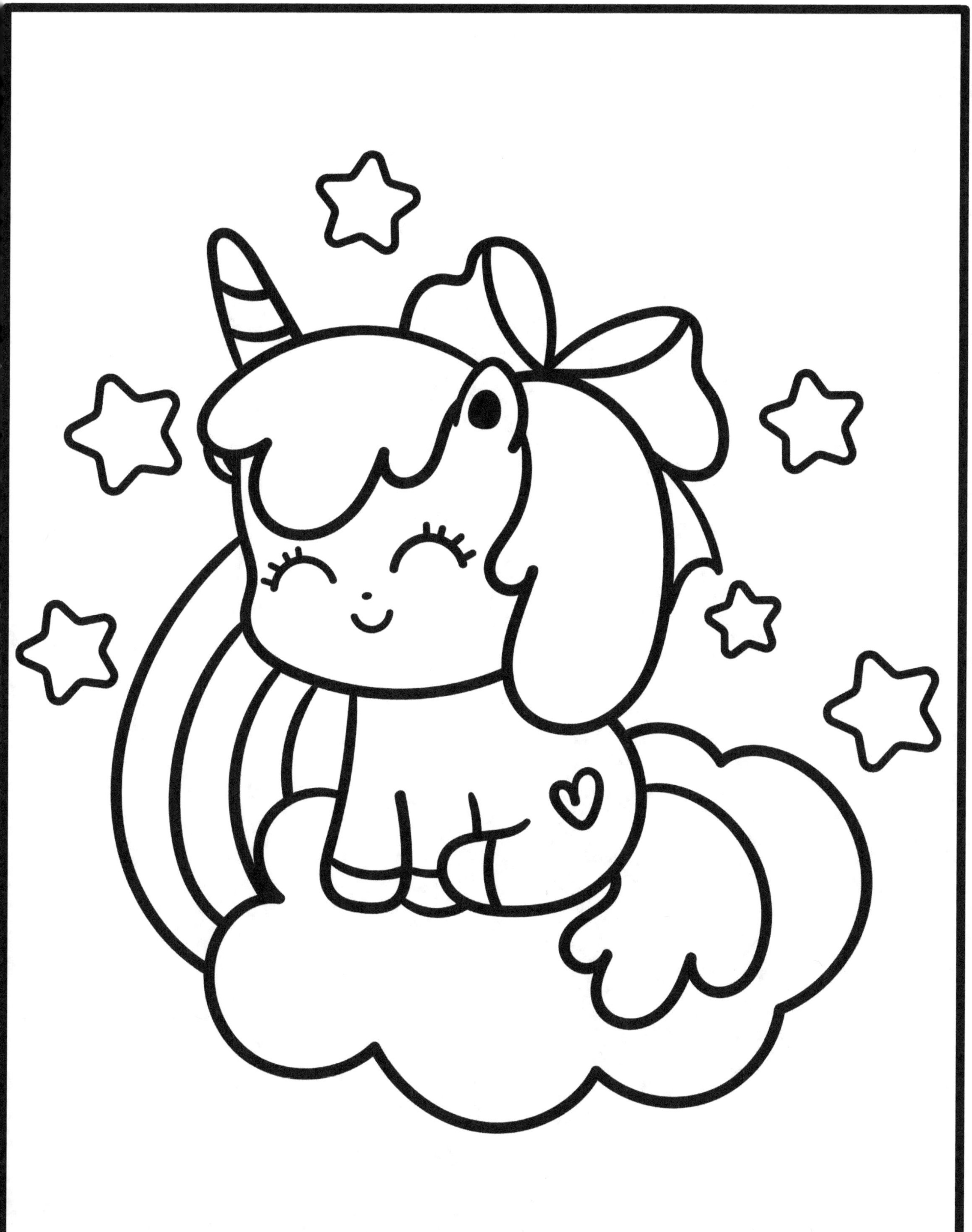

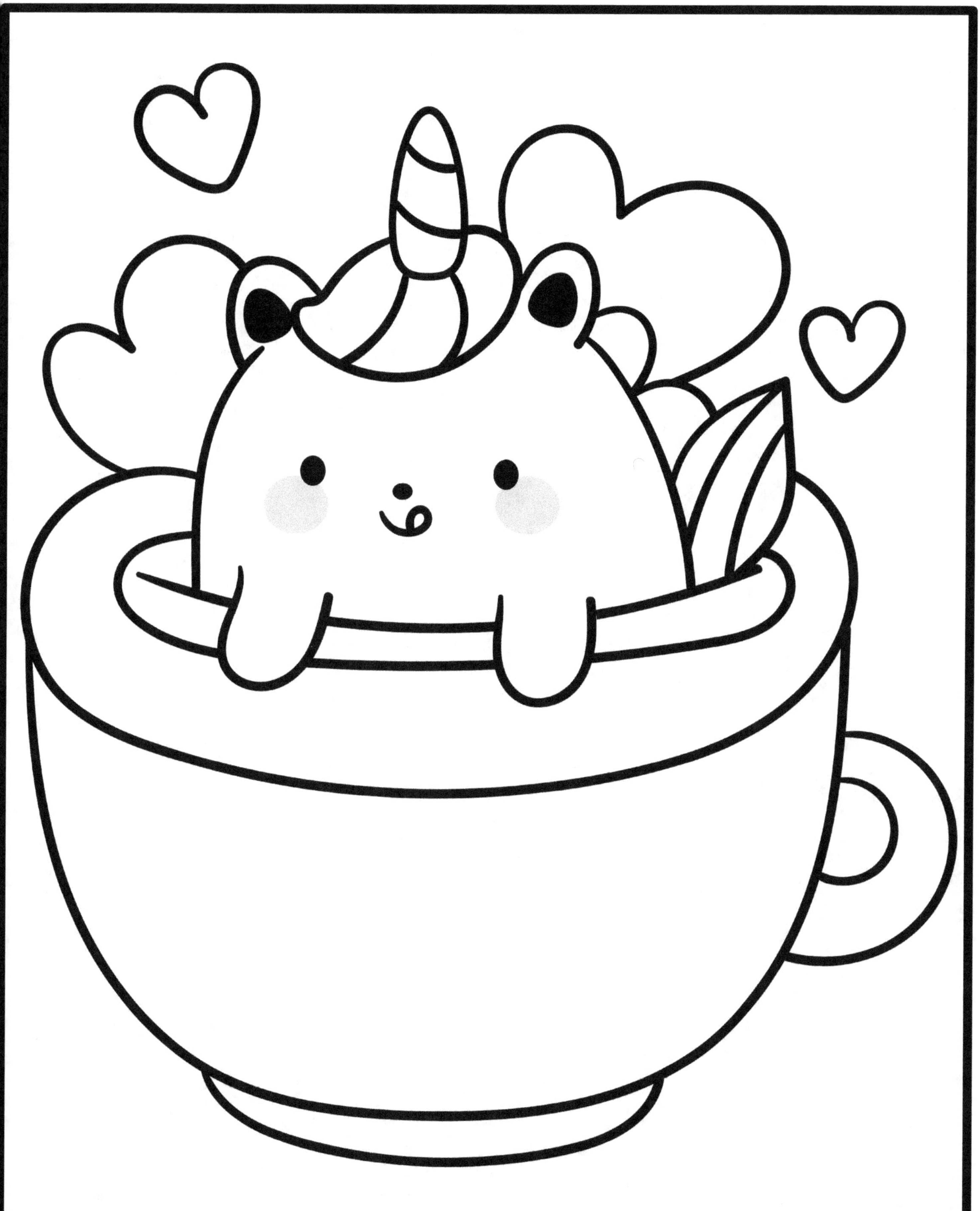

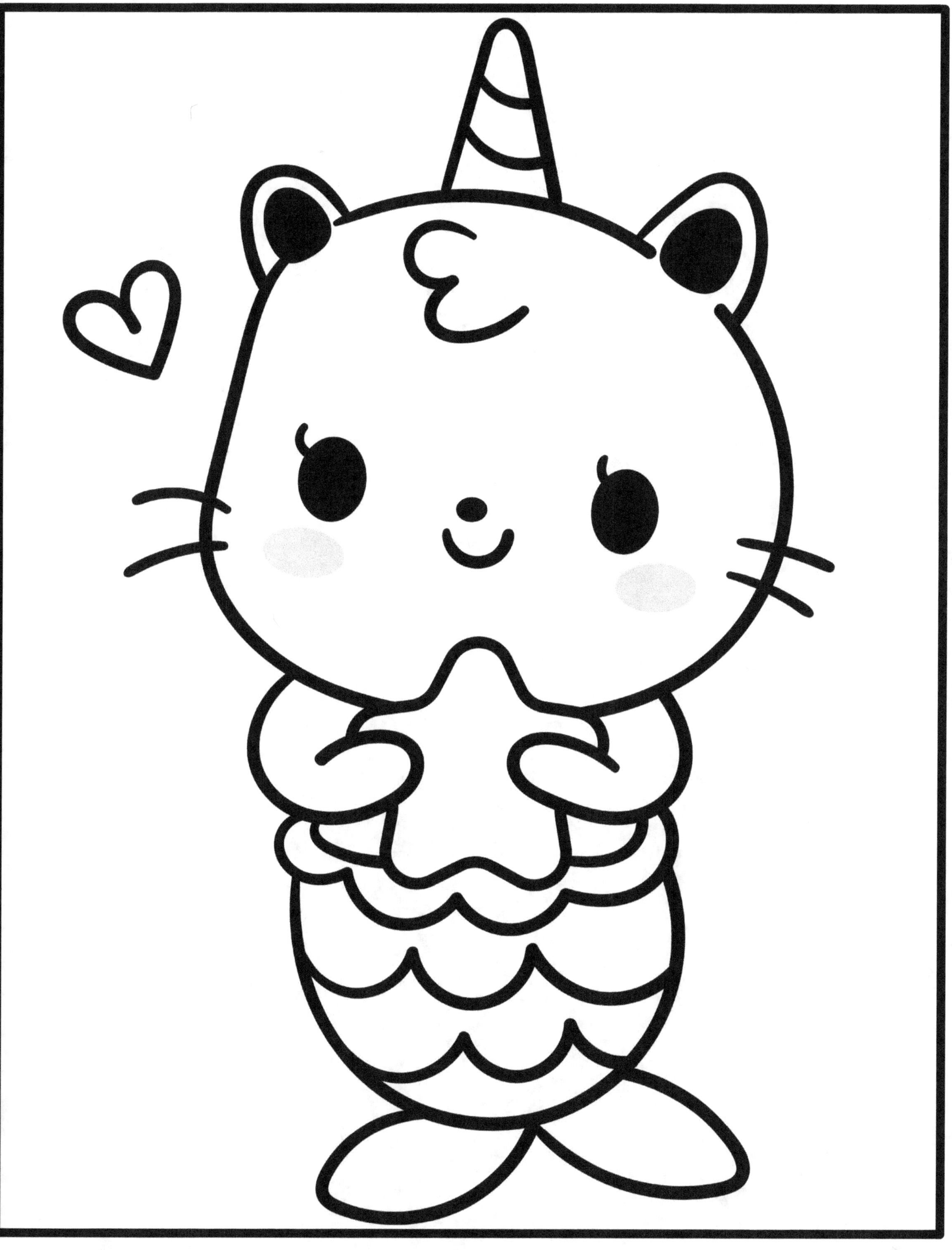

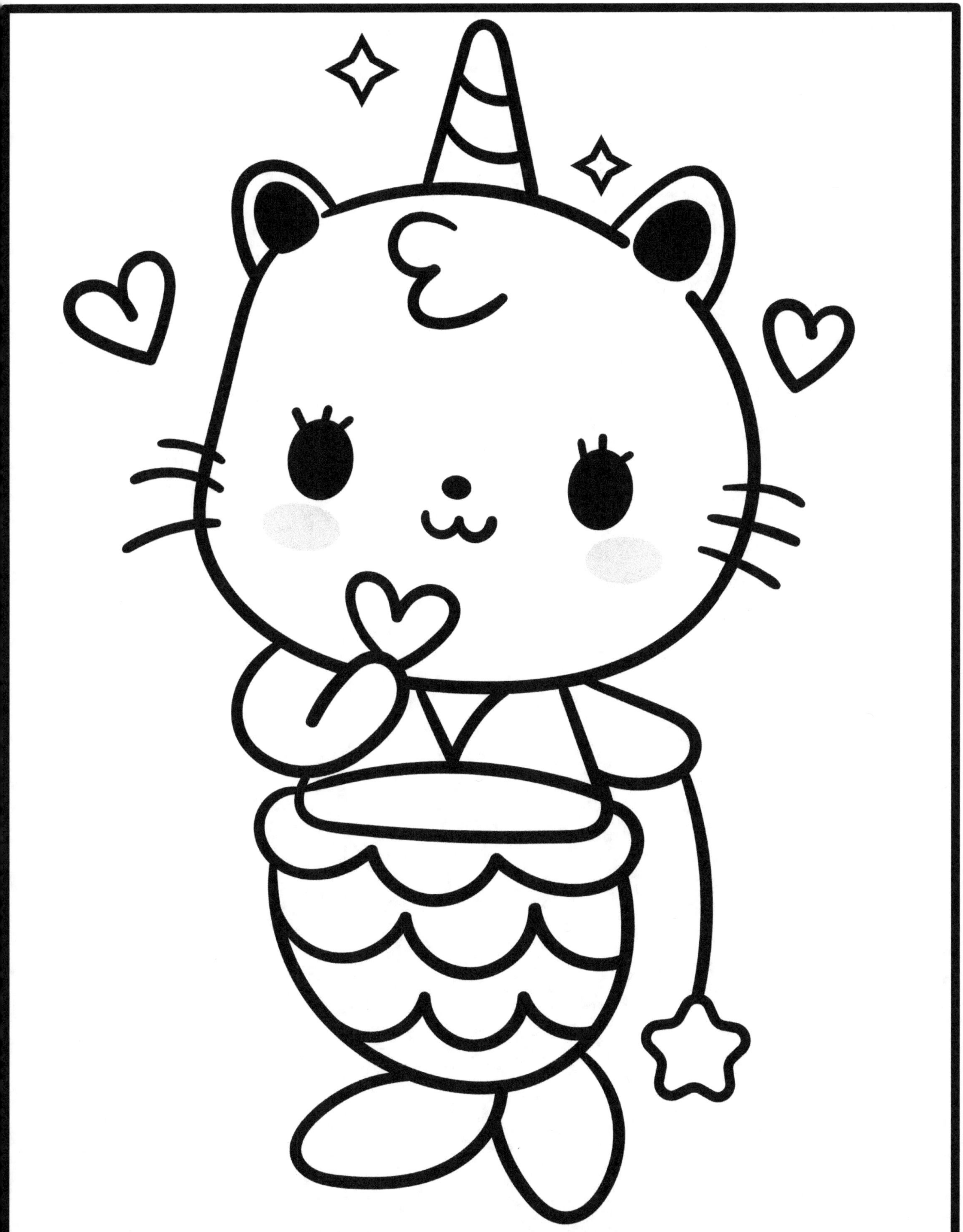

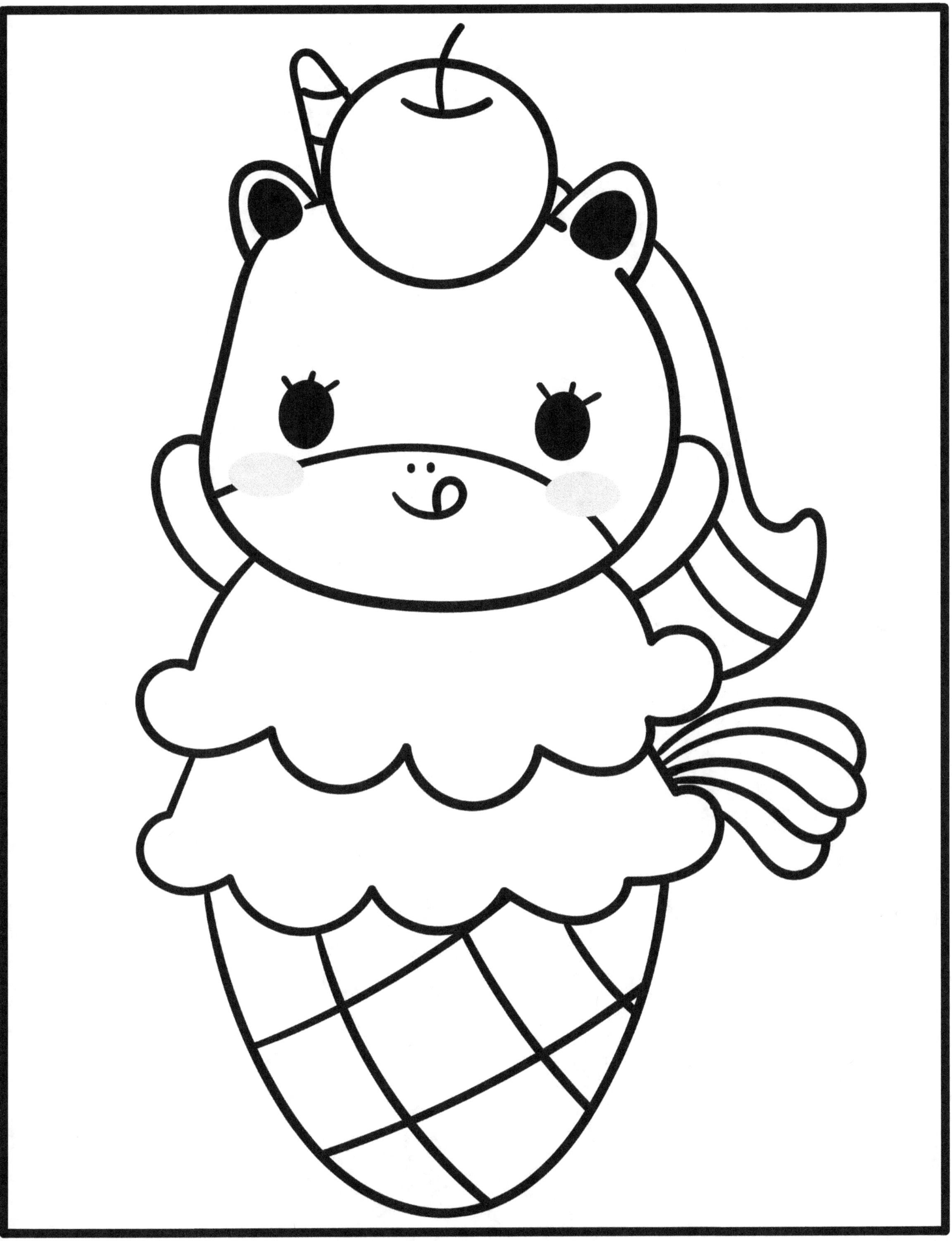

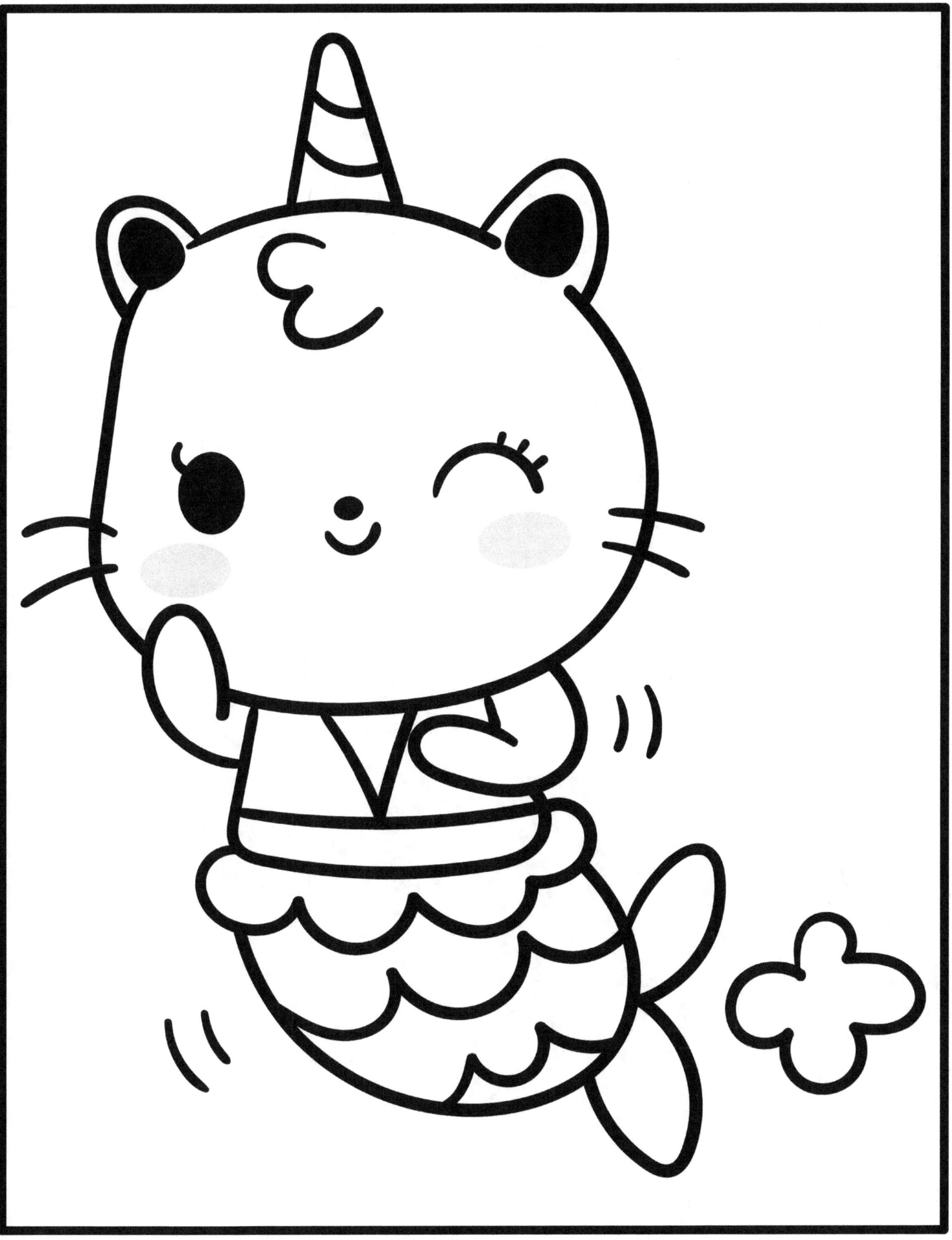

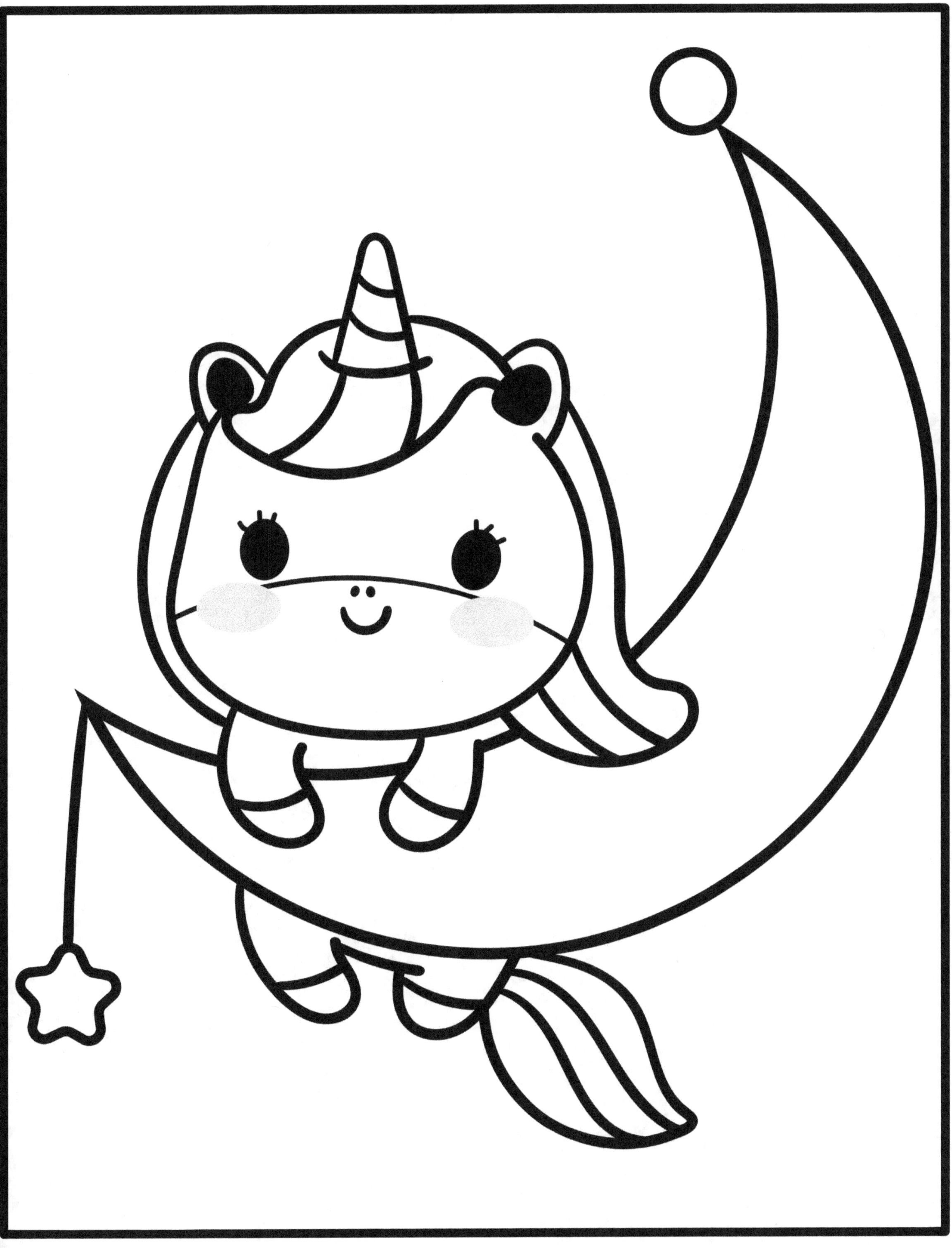

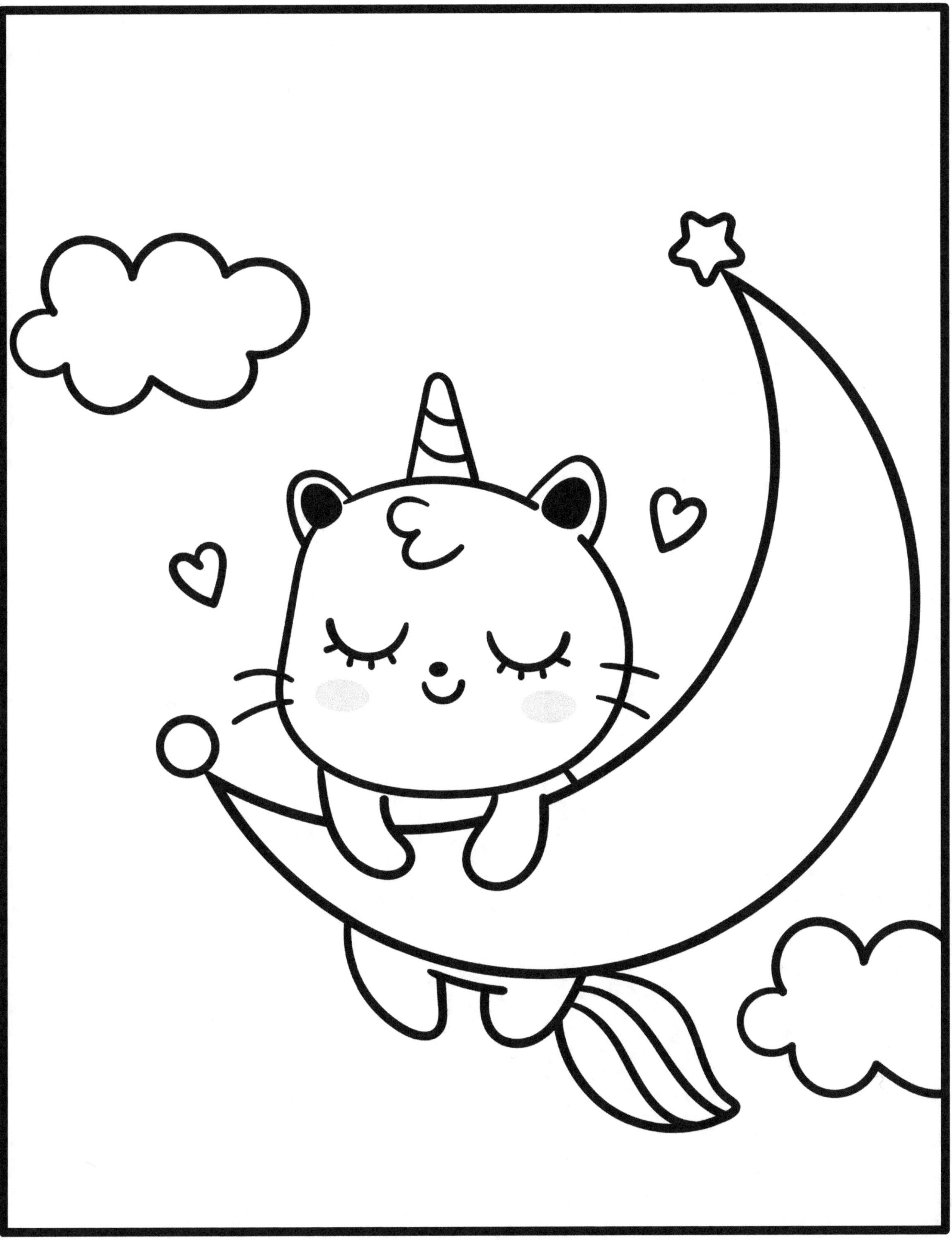

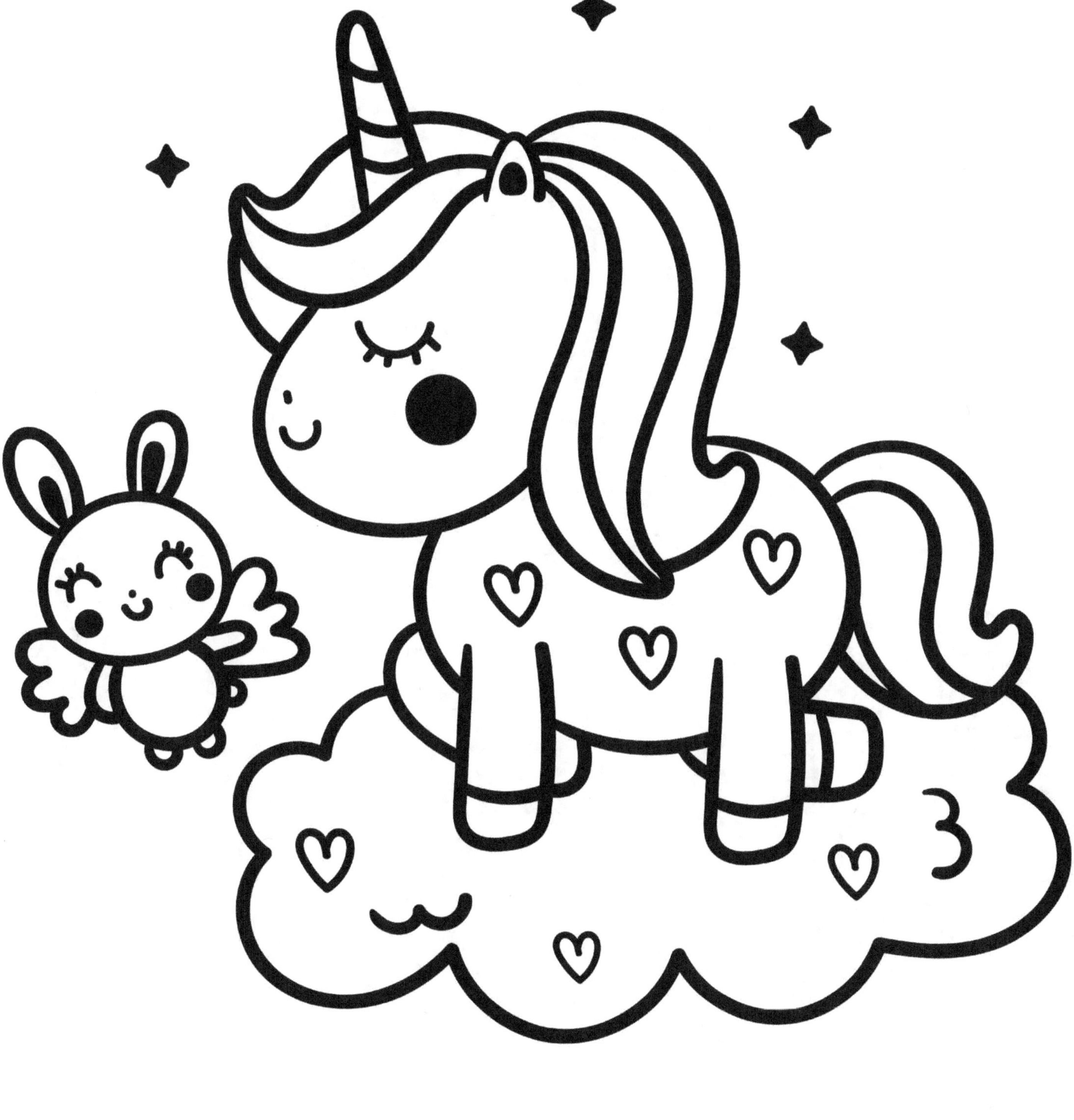

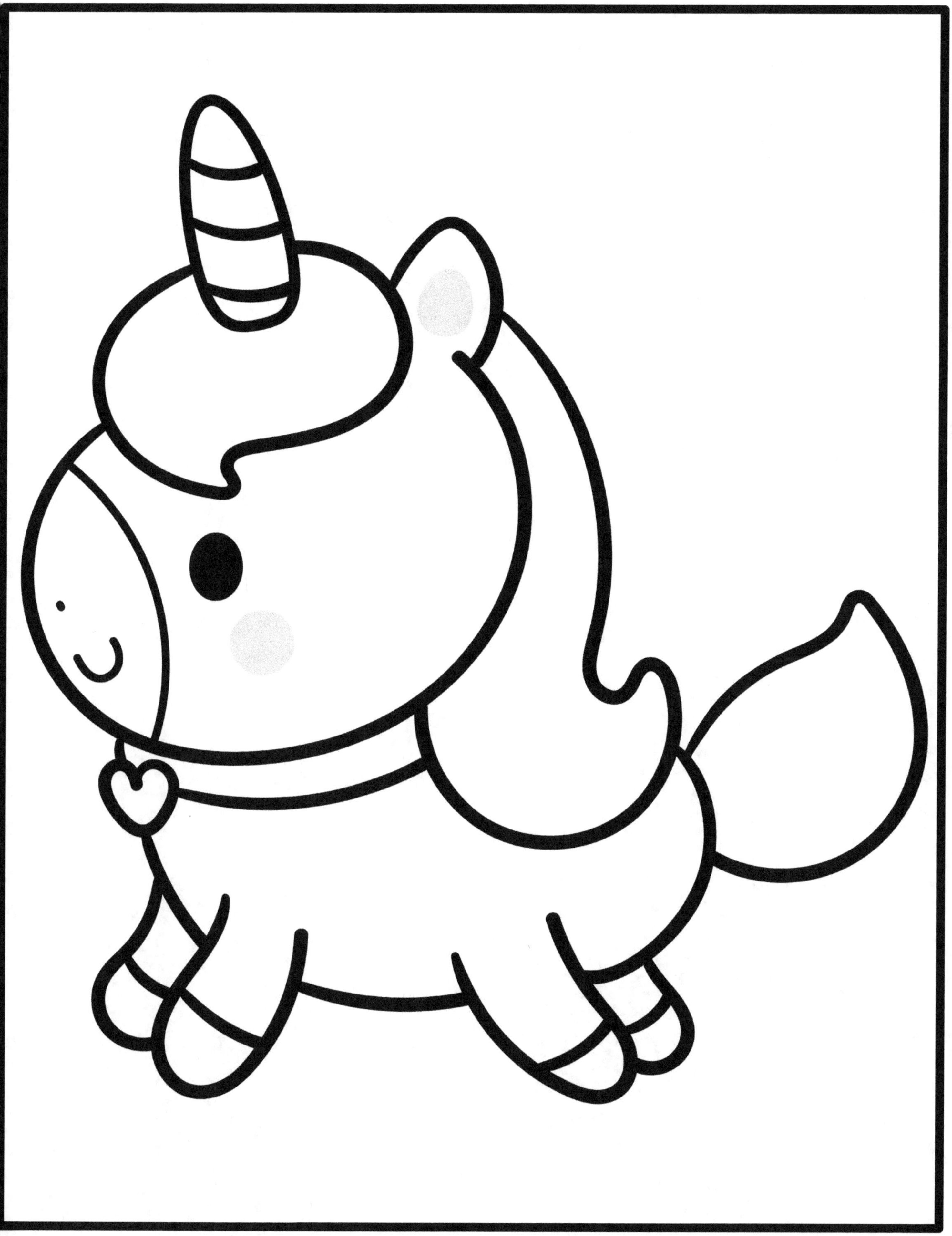

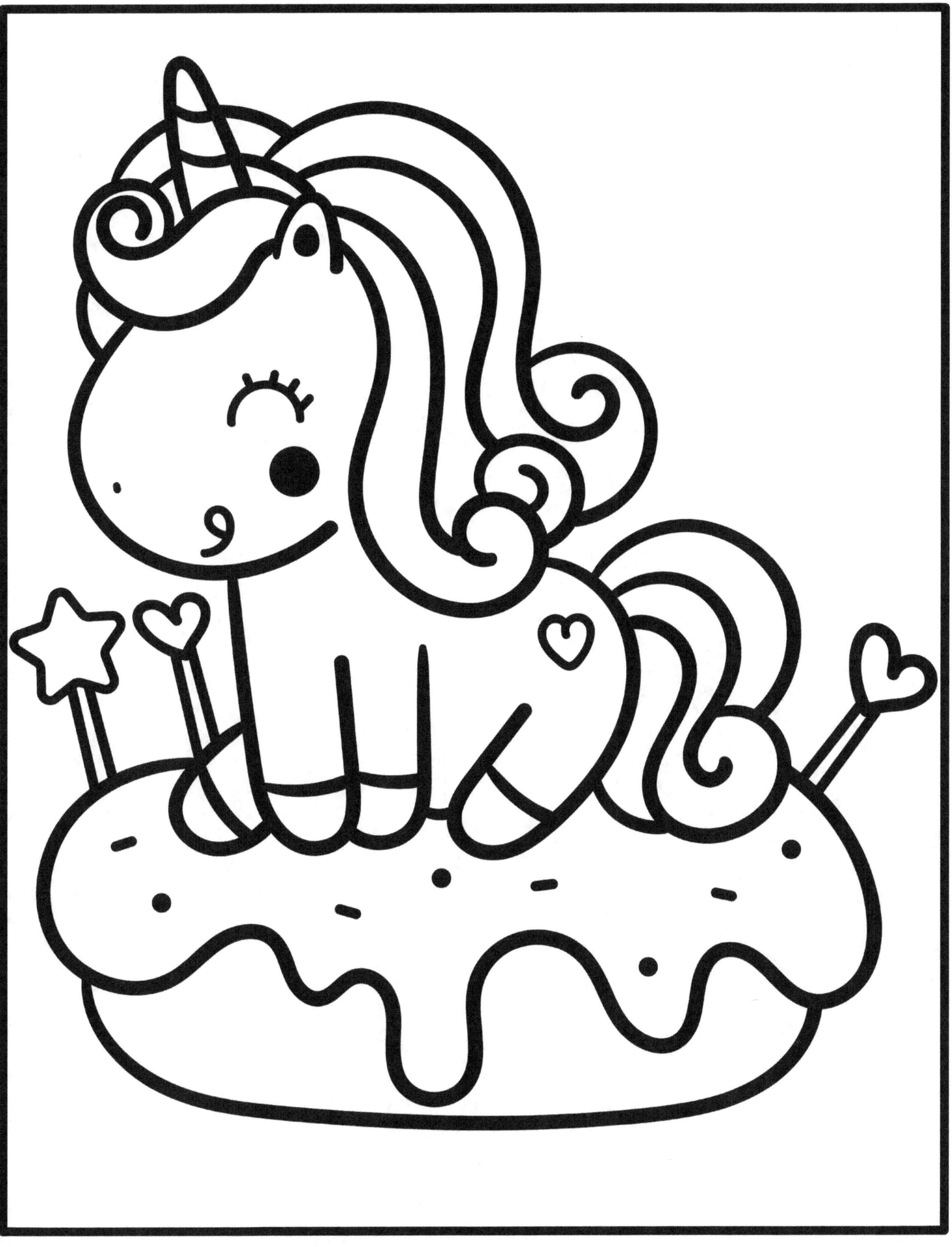

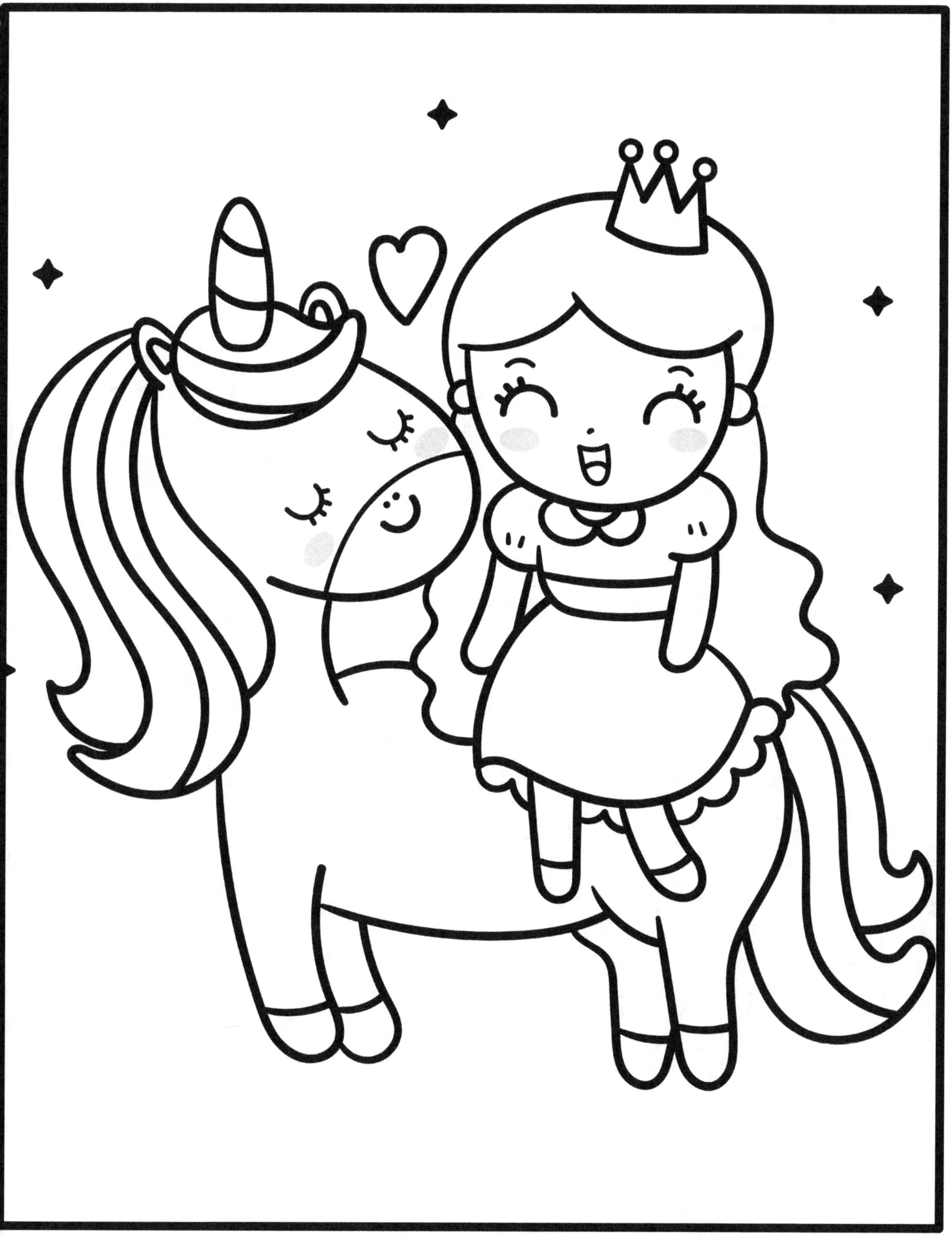

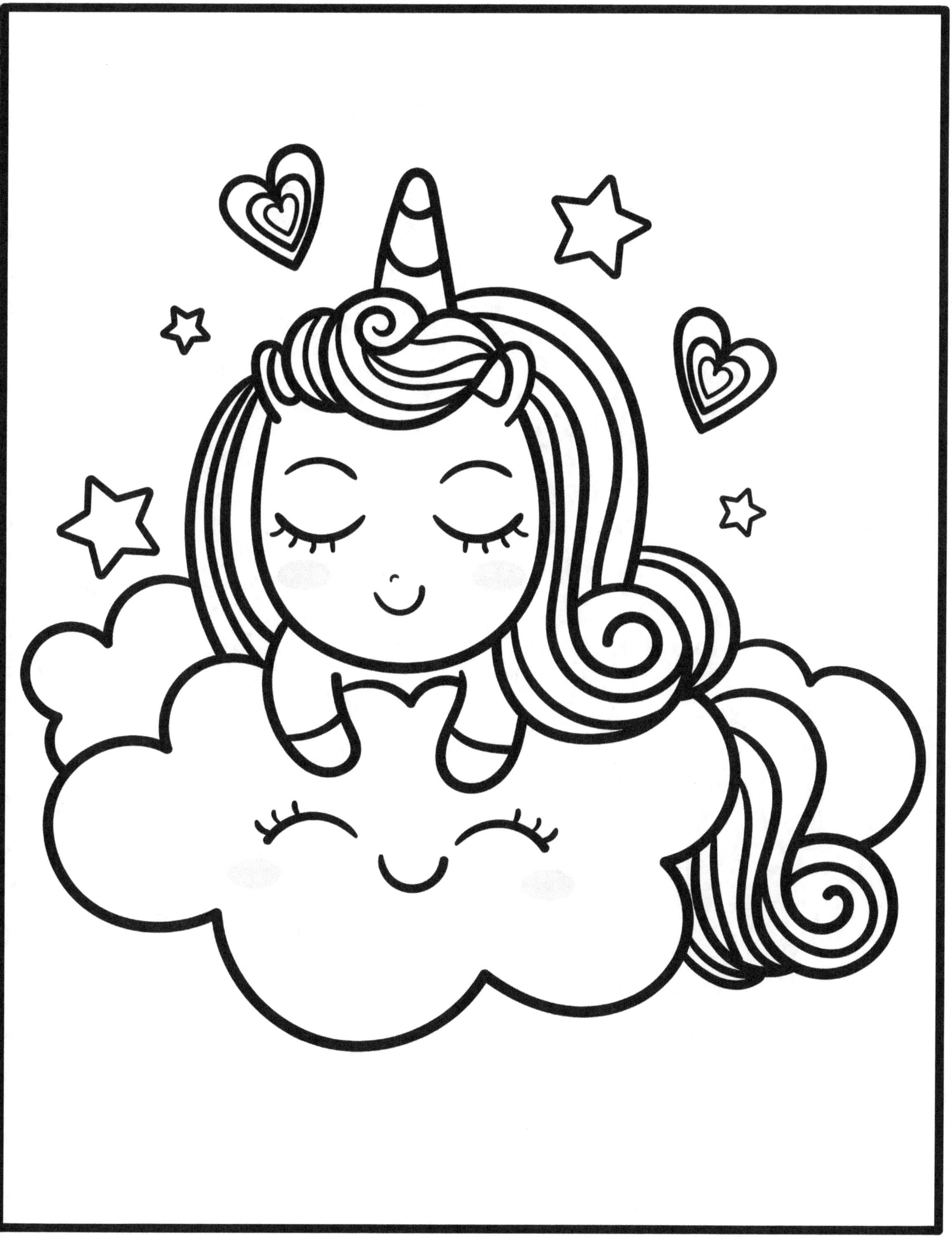

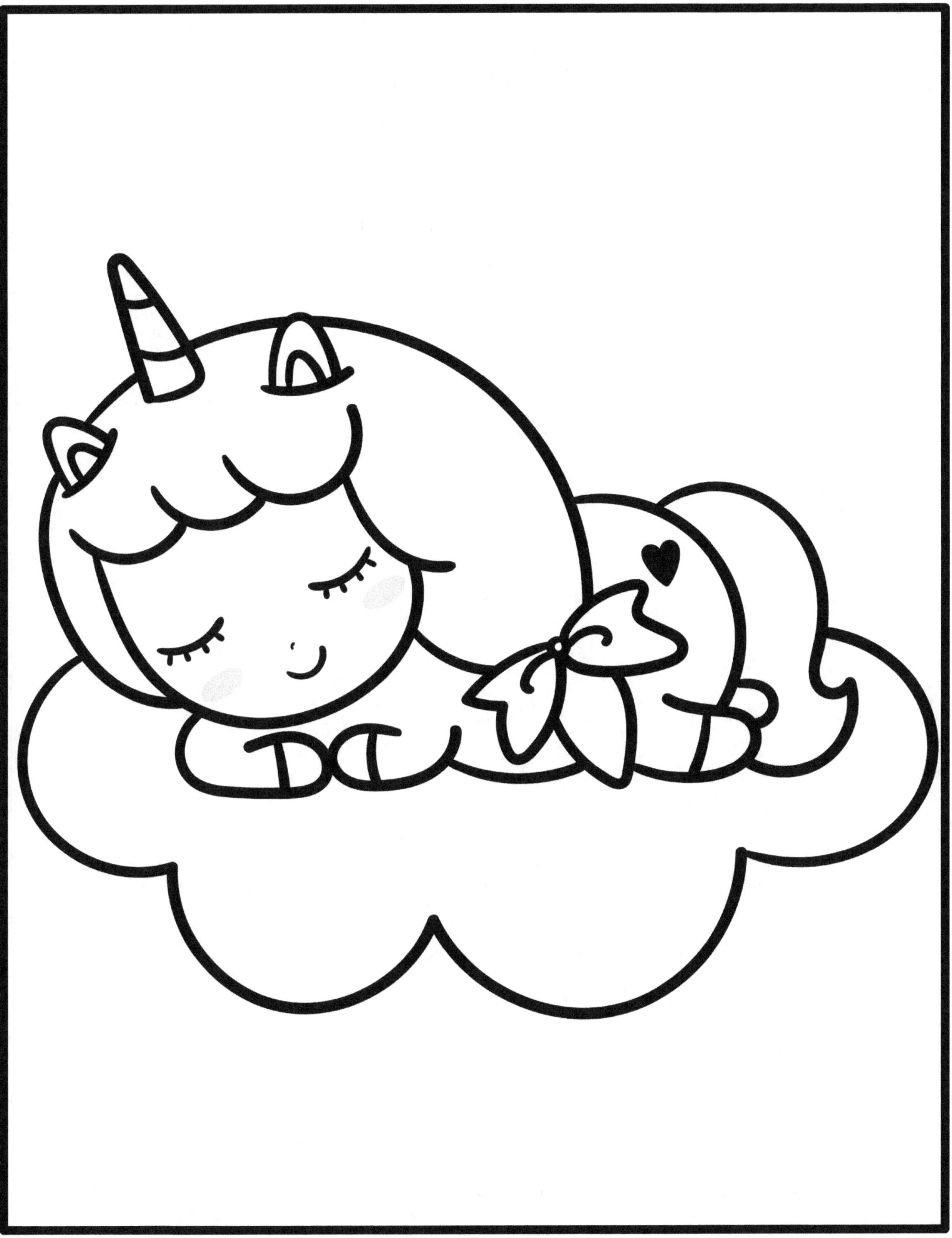

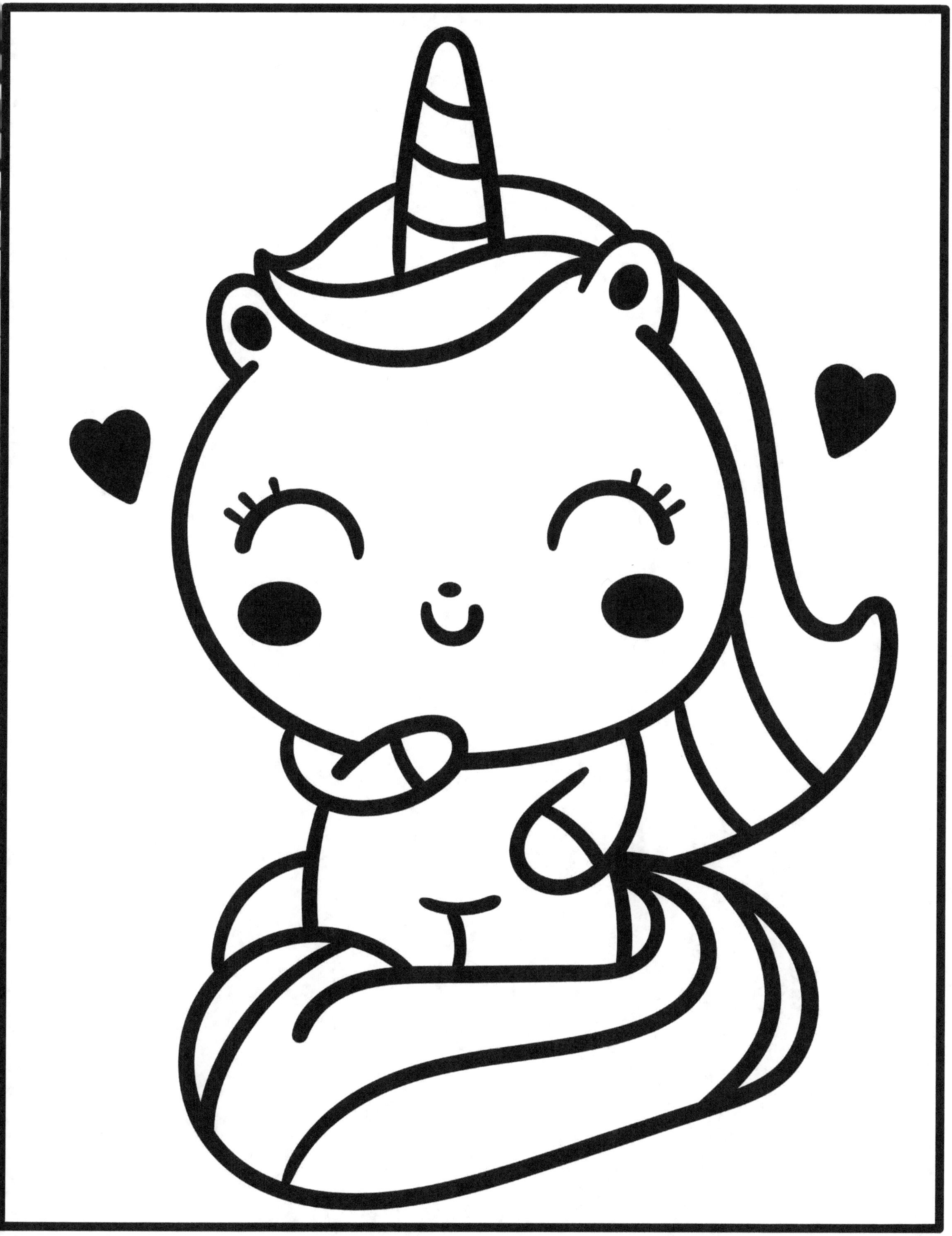

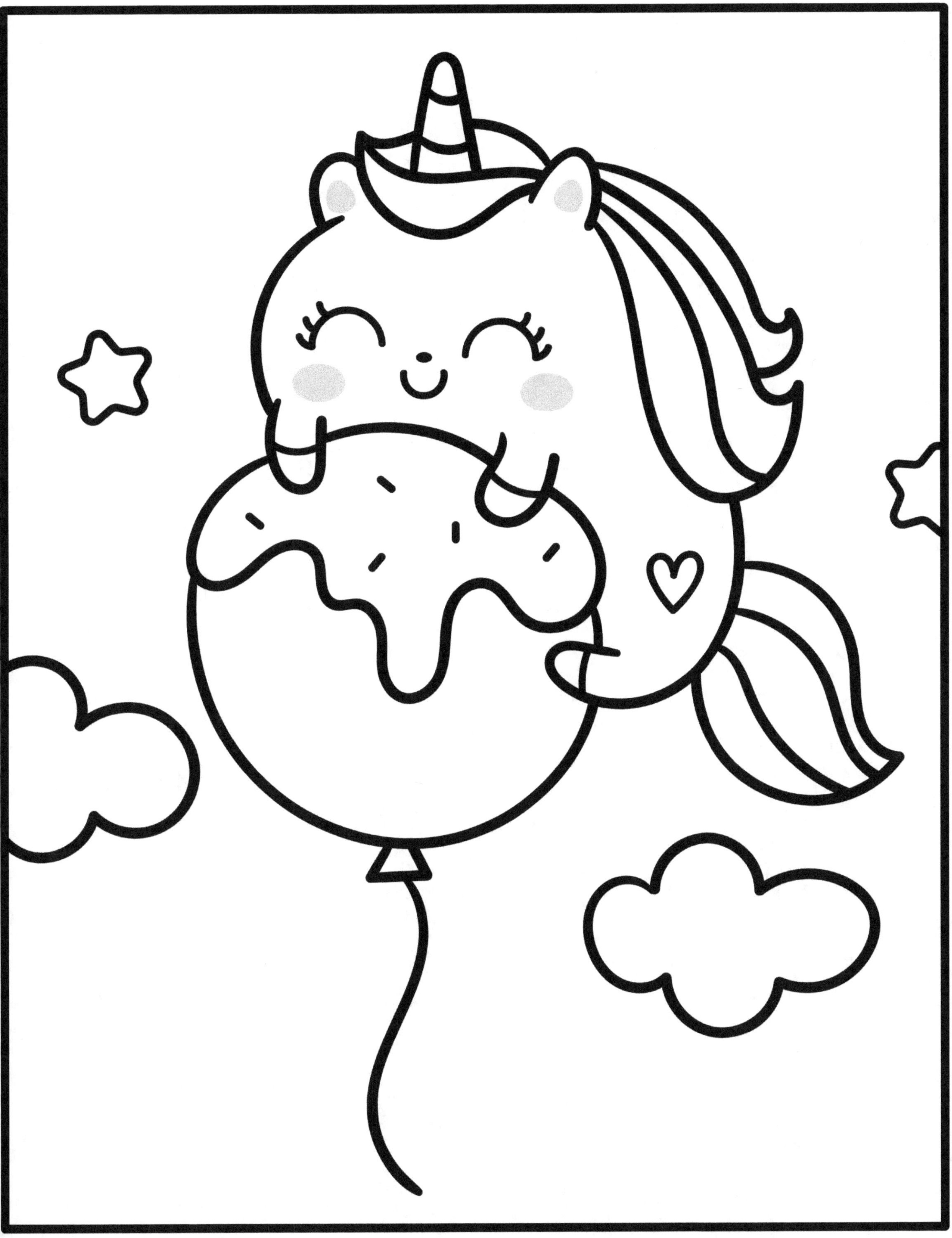

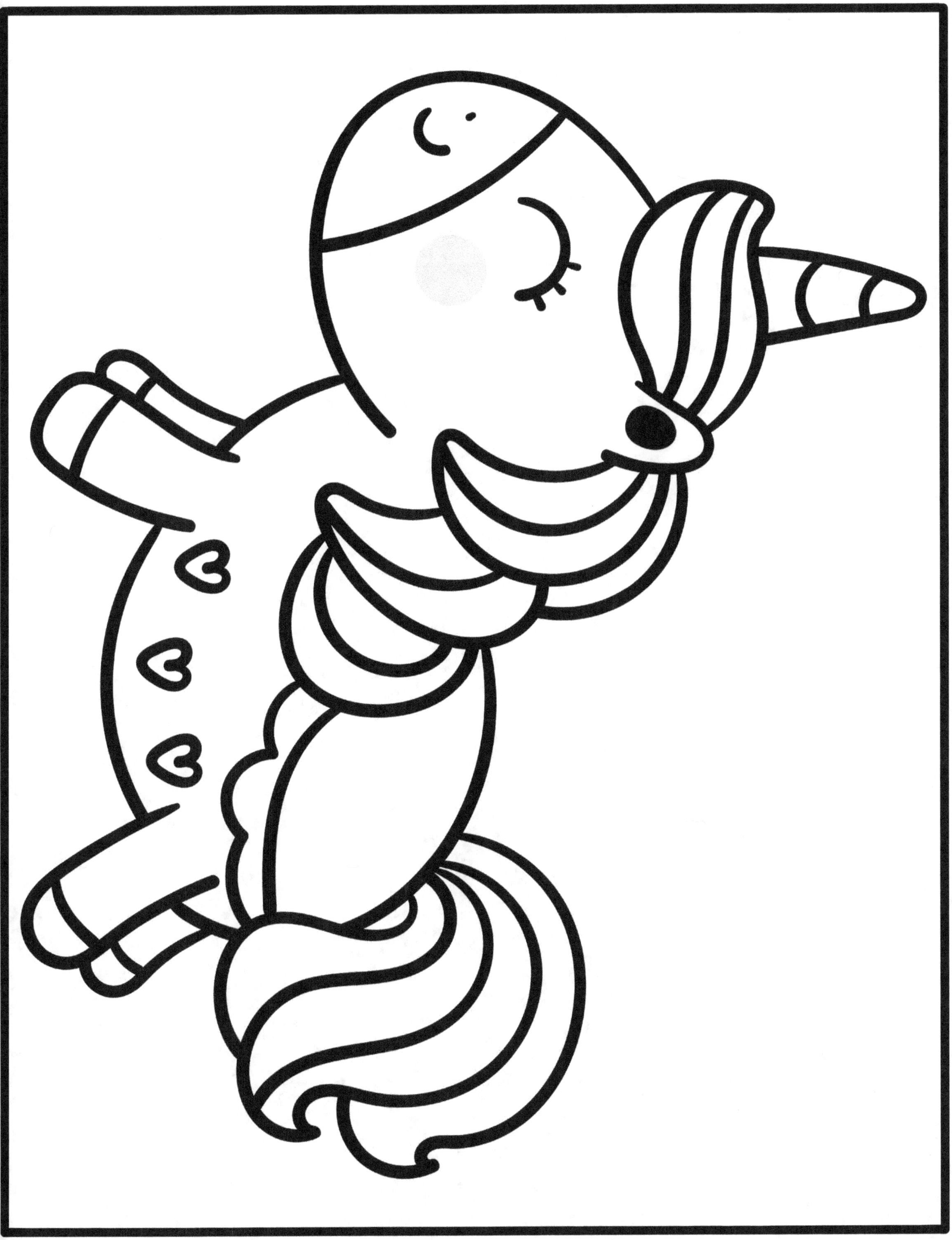

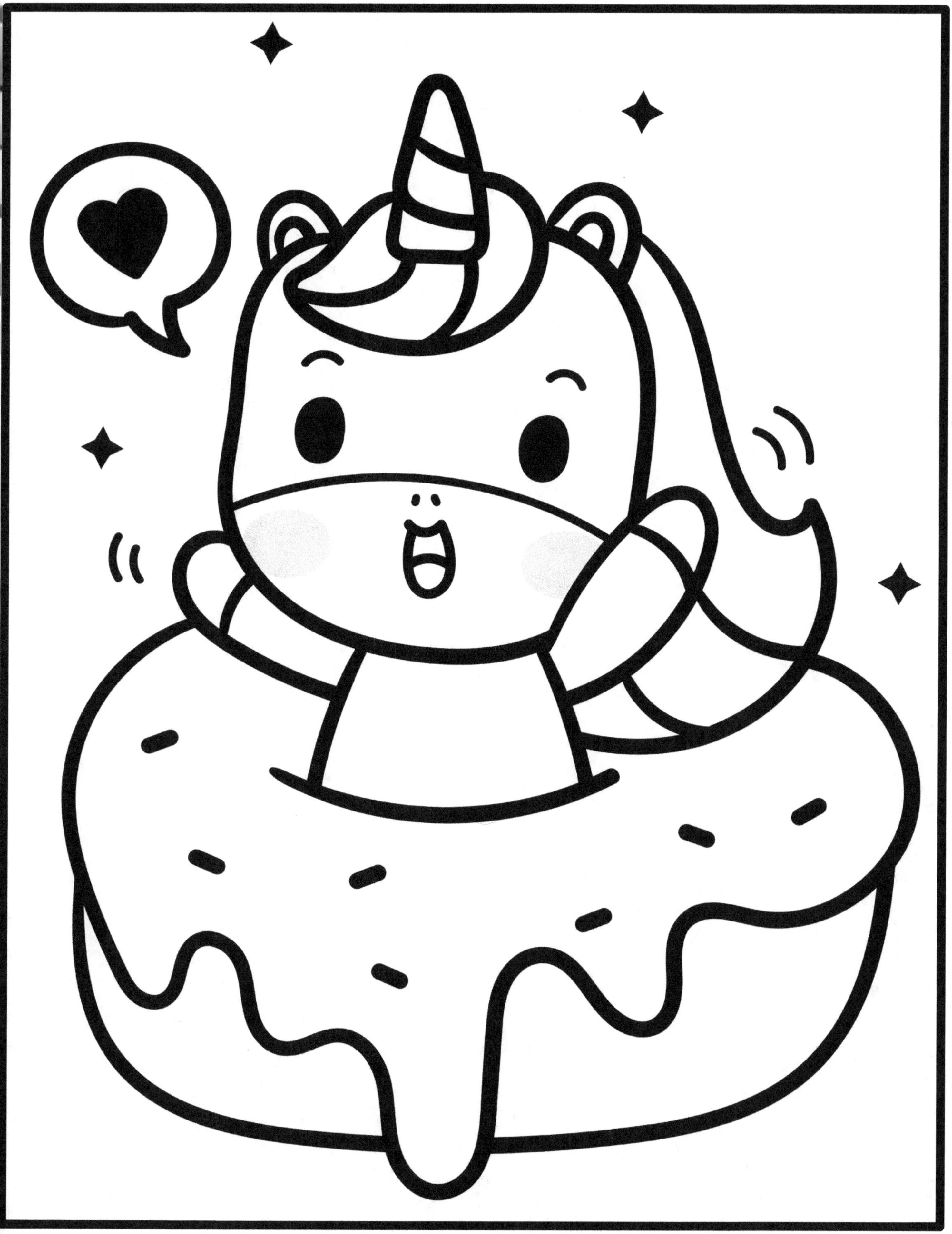

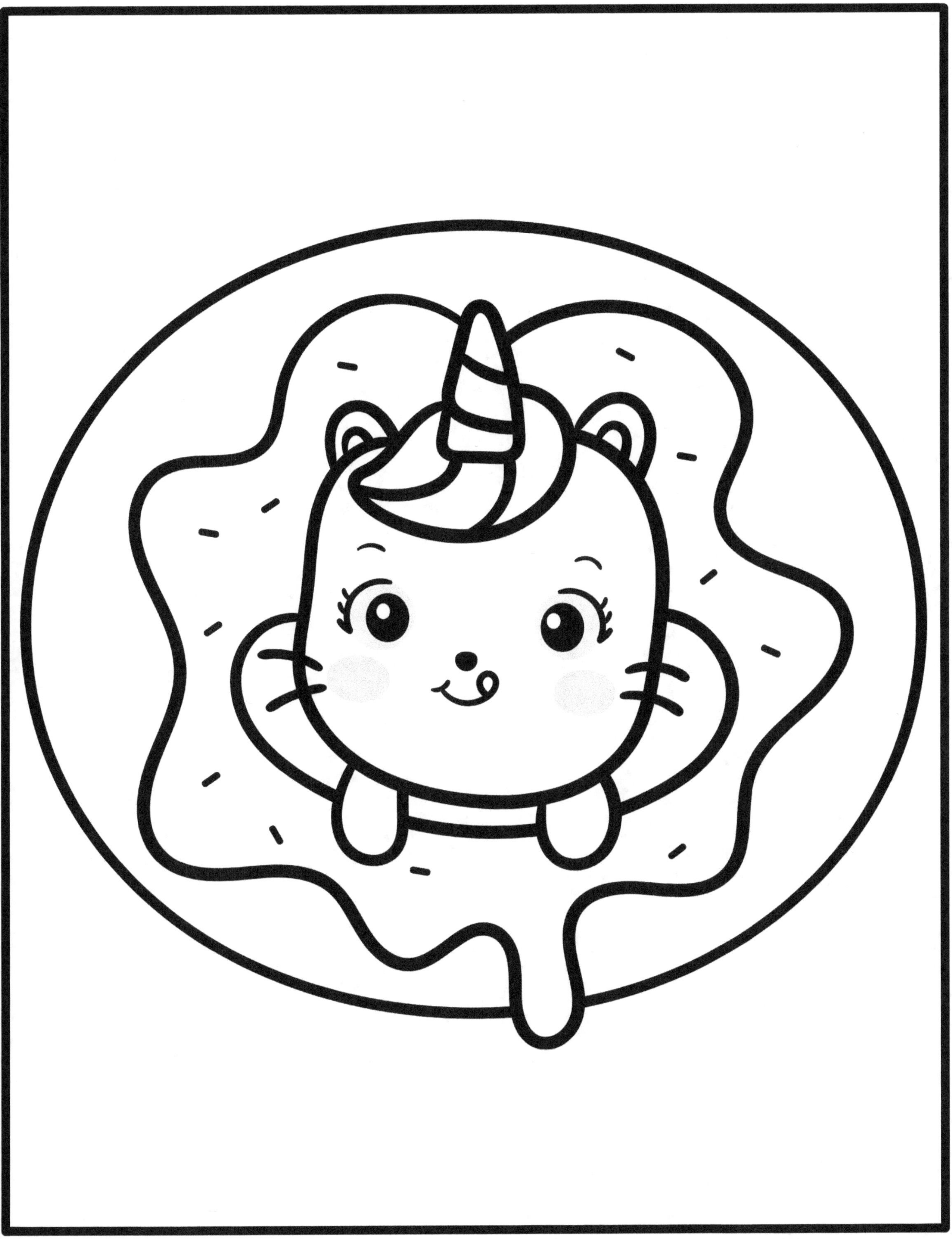

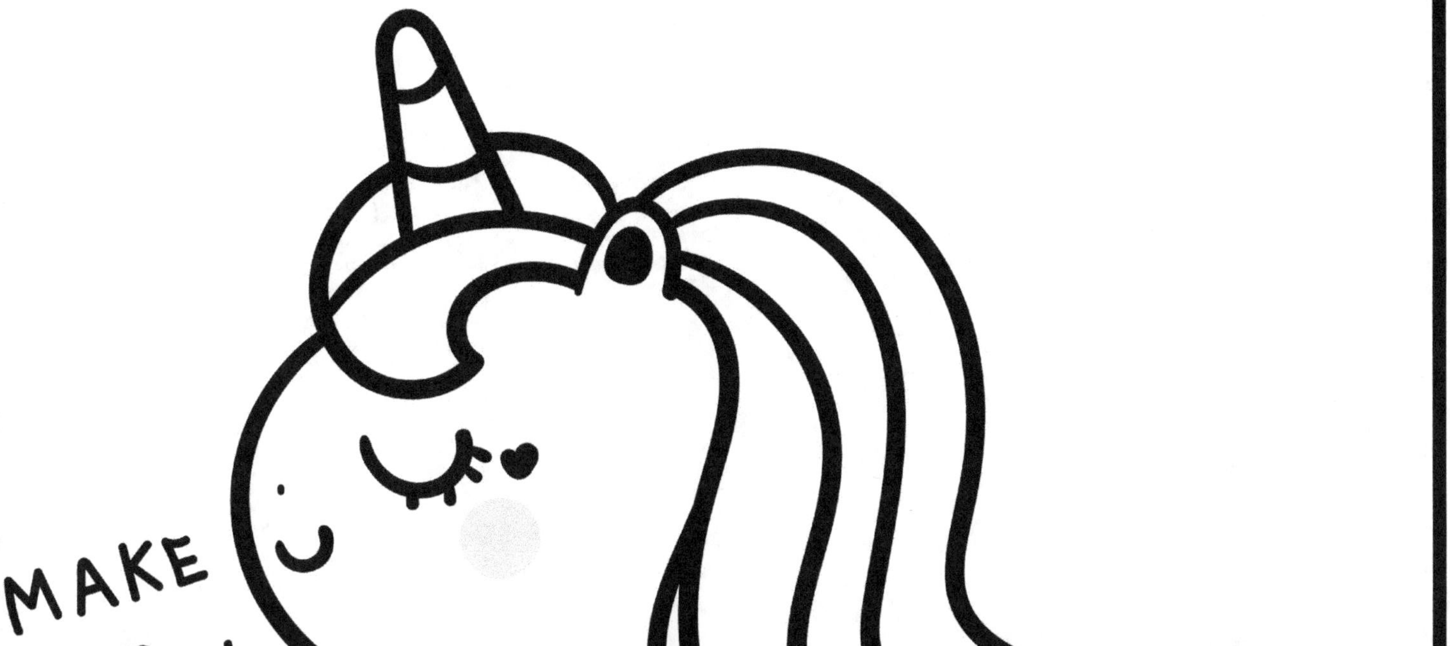
MAKE
A WISH

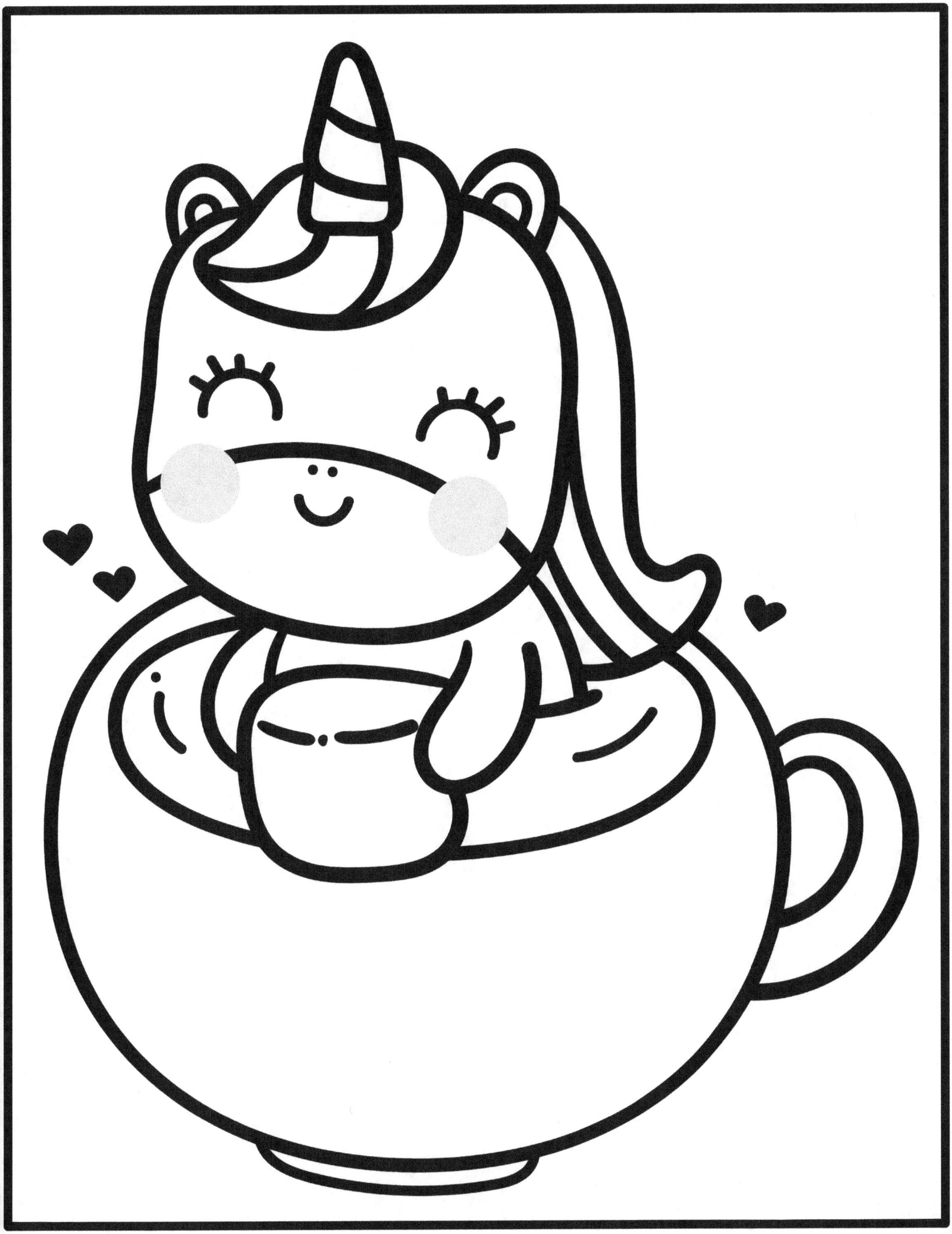

www.ingramcontent.com/pod-product-compliance
Lightning Source LLC
Chambersburg PA
CBHW081433220526
45466CB00008B/2372
9781675055755